The
REAL
JESUS

יֵשׁוּעַ

The
REAL
JESUS

יֵשׁוּעַ

A Revealing Study Based On Ancient Hebrew Writings

By Ronald L Drown

ANCIENT TRUTH PUBLISHING

The Real Jesus

יֵשׁוּעַ

Written By Ronald L Drown

Cover and Design ~ Martha R Grass
Copyright © 2013 Ancient Truth Publishing
International Standard Book Number 978-0-9886616-0-8

ALL RIGHTS RESERVED.

Bible Scripture Quotations Are From:
The King James Version

For More Information Contact:

Ancient Truth Publishing
PO Box 366894, Bonita Springs, FL 34136
www.AncientTruthPublishing.com

Dedication

This book is for the curious seeker of Truth

...Those who are students of the Bible...
Seeking facts about the life of the Jewish Jesus
in regards to history Christianity and Judaism.

...Dedicated to an exceptional few who have a
thirst for knowledge and a yearning to
know the Truth because

"Ye Shall Know The Truth
And The Truth Shall
Make You Free"
(John 8:32)

Table of Contents

Preface

In my earliest teen years, and after my conversion to Christianity, my mind was impressed to read the Christian Bible completely through. I was focused and wanted to learn as much as possible about the faith, and began reading as quickly as I could from Genesis to Revelation. Much of my spare time was spent reading the entire Bible. I knew how important it was, and I figured a way to integrate my Bible reading with my Western Union job as a "messenger boy." In spare moments, while awaiting telegrams to deliver, it became time for Bible reading.

God had laid His hand on my heart, supernaturally giving me a "call to preach," but I also knew that much preparation was needed for the task. Knowing that if ever one was to be a spokesman for God, that person needed to know what God had said, be willing to say it for the people, and have a sense of how to apply the word of God to life and its situations.

The revelation about preaching was what made me want to get "saved." I knew that anyone who spoke on God's behalf had better first "get right with God."

Wanting self assurance that what was being read was also being properly understood was very important to me. So after arriving at that plateau, I recognized, by the grace of God, that along with my Bible, a great study tool was available to assist in even knowing what words meant in the biblical source languages, before they were rendered into English. I purchased a Strong's Exhaustive Concordance of the Bible, with its Hebrew-English Lexicon, and learned how to faithfully use it. The alphabetized concordance in the book, along with its italicized and bold numbering systems linking to Hebrew and Greek words, was a very good tool for learning and study.

Thank God for James Strong. His nurse may have thought the reported messy smoker was a problem, but his monumental work was a Godsend for Christian believers. Strong's Concordance was a must, as a bible companion.

Understanding what certain words and phrases meant in the times of Jesus and the Hebrew prophets, and how to apply them to our times, seemed very appropriate. This began a quest and thirst for biblical knowledge, which continued to be motivated by the Holy Spirit in my life. My mind was illuminated, and enabled as I began some examination of the Hebrew and Greek text copies.

Soon I began to study as well, some Hebrew culture and customs, with long established traditions. After all, I reasoned; *If Jesus taught in Hebrew parables to the people, it would be wise to learn as much of both the Hebrew language, and culture as possible, so as to know the Bible in its original form.* The discipline of "study" with intensity during those early years, has kept my thirst for truth well satisfied, even unto this day.

As years passed and biblical knowledge was gained, I began the study of the Hebrew and Greek languages. My preaching experience as a young man was mostly evangelistic, before years of pastoral work, first as an assistant, and then as pastor. I held almost every possible office to be a blessing when they needed me. My pastor was a very good man and granted many opportunities for growth and ministry.

During the many years as a pastor, I was driven to study harder than ever, and the learning curve began to pay off in big dividends. Congregants who had served the Lord many years would often testify how long they had been in church, but had never heard or learned some of the things I was sharing with them from my studies. They would check the teachings over and over, only to return and admit that they were learning as never before. The flock was being well fed and indeed growing fat.

This introduction is an effort to help you, the reader to also be aware of the importance of research and self study, and to search for and expect good nuggets of truth. You are going to have the joy of sharing the benefit of the things of God, from His word. The calling had been given years before:

> *I charge thee therefore before God, and the Lord Jesus Christ, who shall judge the quick and the dead at his appearing and his kingdom; preach the word, be instant in season, out of season; reprove, rebuke, exhort with all longsuffering and doctrine. For the time will come when they will not endure sound doctrine; but after their own lusts shall they heap to themselves teachers, having itching ears. And they shall turn away their ears from the truth, and shall be turned unto fables. But watch thou in all things, endure afflictions, do the work of an evangelist, make full proof of thy ministry.*

As best I know, I have always been as true as possible to that charge. The Divine order of exhort, reprove, and rebuke, has at times caused me much trouble, but through it all, the grace of God has been sufficient. In that grace I remain standing.

Faithfully Yours,

Pastor Ronald L Drown

Author Note:

It should be made known at the start that, scripture verse references in support of the views and thoughts of the writer, are from the King James Version of the Bible or K.J.V. When other translation versions are available, this will be identified by large capitals [JPS], or explanation of the source will be given.

At the end of this book you will find a Glossary of Terms, (not in alphabetical order but appearing in the same order as chapters develop) created especially for those unfamiliar with Judaism, Sages and historical figures, important writings of influential scholars, and other reference materials which should greatly enhance your study.

Acknowledgements and Gratitude

I wish to thank my wife Ruth for all her patience with me, when I am so busy working on projects. She is such a longsuffering soul, and loving person.

Also a huge debt of gratitude is owed my daughter Martha, for her appreciated assistance in computer formatting for book preparation, as well as the time she spent in developing web sites, marketing, and other business endeavors.

ישוע

and the Synagogue

Chapter 1

Jesus and the Synagogue

The four Christian Gospels give us about twelve references regarding Jesus and attending synagogue. Those sources show that his customs and upbringing was well in line with Orthodox Judaism during the years of his youth and childhood, as well as during approximately three years of ministry. One of the Gospel examples is found in Luke 4:16, (King James Version Bible), which says:

> *And He came to Nazareth, where he had been brought up; and as his custom was, He went into the synagogue on the Shabbat day, and stood up for to read.*

That verse pretty much shows the habit, custom, and upbringing of Jesus before and after his adult life, and his religious observance pattern.

The next verse (vs.17) reveals that the scroll of Isaiah was given to Jesus and he stood and read from a place or particular section after he found it. Standing when one reads from the Hebrew Bible is a custom yet in practice today. People stand when reading from the Torah in honor of the sacred word of God. Twelve references show that in synagogues he taught the people on Shabbat (Sabbath)

שַׁבָּת

and he also healed the sick and expelled demons in the synagogue on the Shabbat.

I cite the verse locations here for serious students: Matthew 12:9, Matthew 13:54, Mark 1:21, Mark 3:1, Mark 6:2, Luke 4:15, Luke 4:16, Luke 4:33, Luke 6:6, Luke 13:10, John 6:59, John 18:20.

Jesus was a Jew, and as such, and in that setting, he lived, and observed until the day of his death

Christians should realize that the leader of their faith was a faithful observant Jew (even as youth).

It seems difficult for Christian's to hear that the man Jesus never attended church. But when we realize the biblical sources about his life, it's quite clear that he attended a "synagogue."

What is a synagogue? It is the normal place of worship for the Jew, since the Temple no longer is operational. Yiddish speakers use the term "shul" (*school*) instead of synagogue.

The Greek term "*sunago*" (A Concordance # 4863), *means, to lead together, to collect or convene, which is farther explained as an assemblage of persons.*

In a limited sense, it is similar to the Greek term that was rendered "church," which is (*ekklhsia*), and was used by Christians for their houses of gathering to worship, but was not a reference to the building, rather to the people. Jews do not use the term church to refer to their houses of worship and study.

A prophecy by Ezekiel, in chapter 11 and verse 16, that mentions the scattering of Israel and inhabitants of Jerusalem far off among the heathen, has strong indication that synagogues or shuls may be "little sanctuaries."

> *Although I have scattered them among the countries, yet will I be to them as a little sanctuary in the countries where they shall come.*

The Hebrew term for little sanctuaries is

l'mikdash meh'at

לְמִקְדָּשׁ מְעַט

The root for mikdash is the same term used elsewhere in the Hebrew Bible for the Holy Tabernacle, when God told Moses and Israel to make for Him a sanctuary that He may dwell among them. (Exodus 25:8)

מִקְדָּשׁ

Thus, the term "little sanctuary" (King James Version Bible), may have prophetic significance in that it relates to synagogues. Judaism has continued despite loss of Temple, or exile of Jews, and although the Temple yet existed in the time of Jesus, there also existed in Jerusalem about 460 or 480 synagogues, according to exaggerated Jewish traditions. Another thought...

If Jesus attended synagogues throughout Israel during his time, when did he attend them?

ANCIENT HEBREW WISDOM

ALL THAT GOD DOES
IS DONE FOR THE BEST

(Ber. 60^b; D. 452).
Ancient Sacred Text

ישוע

and the

Sabbath (Shabbat)

Holy Days

Chapter 2

Jesus and the Sabbath (Shabbat) Holy Days

Our 12 sources in the Christian Gospels clarify that it was on a "sabbath" day.

What is Sabbath?

In Hebrew, the correct transliteration is "*shabbat*." The word (Sabbath) was taken by English translators from the Greek, rather than the Hebrew sources. Thus the "sh" sound is missing (shabbat/sabbath). It means to cease or rest. God ceased from all the work which He had done after the six creative days.

In Genesis 2:2, it was written that God rested on the seventh day from all his work which He had made. The seventh day was blessed and hallowed because He had finished creation relative to humankind, earth and its needs.

God did not rest because He was tired.

Isaiah 40:28 teaches us:

> *Hast thou not known? Hast thou not heard that the everlasting God, the Lord, the Creator of the ends of the earth, fainteth not neither is weary? There is no searching of his understanding.*

A special memorial of creation was established by the Lord. A day of rest... Exodus 20:8 picks up the theme;

"Remember the Sabbath day to keep it holy."

זָכוֹר אֶת־יוֹם
הַשַּׁבָּת לְקַדְּשׁוֹ

That particular day was hallowed by the Lord Himself. Not only do the Ten Commandments mention that Gods name is holy, but they also express that a certain day is holy.

Elsewhere, in Exodus 31:16-17, the Sabbath is said by the Lord, to be a symbol of His covenant with Israel, throughout *"their generations for a perpetual covenant."* It was said to be "a sign" between God and the children of Israel for ever. Jesus, being raised by a Jewish mother and familiar with the Hebrew Bible, was well aware of these teachings.

> *Six days may work be done; but in the seventh is the sabbath of rest, holy to the Lord: whosoever doeth any work in the sabbath day, he shall surely be put to death. Wherefore the children of Israel shall keep the sabbath, to observe the sabbath throughout their generations, for a perpetual covenant.*

Since the Christian Bible wrote in 1Peter 2:22, that Jesus was sinless, and had no deceit in his mouth, we safely assert that he kept the shabbat, and observed all Jewish laws as handed down by Moses and the elders. *What else would we expect of a good and observant Jew?*

We have discussed Jesus and Judaism related to the Sabbath Day, Synagogue, and will soon mention Circumcision. All of those are Jewish subjects and mentioned to some extent in New

Testament source documents with involvement of Jesus.

I want to mention another important subject which is Passover Observance as related in Luke 2:41-42. The text says that every year his parents went to the Feast of the Passover in Jerusalem. We read that his parents observed the "custom," and that Jesus was 12 years old at the time.

God had commanded Moses in Exodus 23:14:

> *"Three times thou shalt keep a*
> *feast unto Me in the year."*

The next verses reveal that Unleavened Bread/Passover, Feast of Weeks, and Tabernacles were the three. The Hebrew terms are *"shalosh regalim,"* and in English are named "Pilgrim Festivals". Other names those feasts are known by are

פֶּסַח, שָׁבוּעוֹת, סֻכּוֹת

Passover, Pentecost, and Sukkot.

While a twelve year old boy, Jesus was yet learning and established in the practice of the Jewish religion of his day. He celebrated Passover with his family. In today's world, he would have been approaching the time of a Bar Mitzvah ceremony, and becoming a "son of the commandment." Mister Edersheim had written; "the legal age in this respect [for Bar Mitzvah] was anticipated by two years or at least by one."

Accepting the yoke of the kingdom of Heaven, and choosing to obey God's every teaching, was part of the 12 year old eagerness and willingness to become a mature adult. The normal Bar Mitzvah age was 13 years and one day, but Jesus during Passover in the Temple at twelve years of age, sat amidst the "*didaskalos*" (Greek for teachers), questioning, and amazing them with answers. In later years during his ministry, he still observed Passover.

Mark 14:12 mentions a Passover meal wherein his disciples killed the lamb and prepared the meal at a selected guestchamber. It was in a large upper room, and the account tells how they broke and blessed the bread and ate. They also drank from the fruit of the vine, and then sang a hymn (Psalm.) Some Christians call this the "last supper," but there is no doubt that it was a celebration of the Passover. It was his last earthly Passover celebration.

The original Passover was intended to memorialize the deliverance of the nation of Israel from Egypt, and it was to be celebrated once every year at a specified calendar date. It took place during a time when Jews were permitted to eat only unleavened bread for seven days. Jesus celebrated it every year once a year. It is nice to know that Jesus attended about 30 Passovers, before he even began a public ministry.

In Mark 14 after his final earthly Passover celebration, Jesus said this in Mark 14:25;

> *Amen, I say unto you, I will drink no more of the fruit of the vine, until that day that I drink it new in the Kingdom of God.*

Thus, the twofold celebration of Passover for the Christian is linked to Israel's deliverance from Egypt, and symbolic of Christ's body and lifegiving blood for the church of God.

But a modern Church often stresses its own notion of Passover celebration rather than the first *Pesach* purpose, which causes loss of the foundational and original meaning.

Parables, and symbols or metaphors, only have real meaning when something is laid alongside a literal truth. A whole nation was delivered from death and bondage, when death skipped over homes where the lamb's blood was applied.

The Passover message was truly Israel's own national miracle, just as much as the body and blood of Christ in Christian theology brings life to repentant and believing sinners.

We should celebrate what God has done at the Passover meal, and on both Jewish and Christian counts.

ישוע

and *Circumcision*

Chapter 3

Circumcision

Another evidence of the Jewishness of Jesus, and also revealing his background and upbringing, is recorded by the author of Luke's Gospel, concerning his actual circumcision [baby Jesus]. Circumcision was a sign of the covenant established long before the Law of Moses had been given at Sinai.

In Genesis 17:10, the Lord had appeared unto Abraham, saying;

> *This is My covenant which ye shall keep, between Me and you and thy seed after thee; every man child among you shall be circumcised.*

Genesis 17:12 wrote that at the early age of eight days and throughout all generations, every man child of Abram's lineage be circumcised.

The Hebrew phrase is

בְּרִית מִלָה

(*berit milah*)

and it literally defines the covenant cut. The circumcision must take place on the 8th day, even if it falls on a Sabbath.

There is some reason for an exception to circumcision, in a case where two family members have died because of excessive loss of blood (*hemophilia*).

Luke 2:21 gives the account of the berit milah of Jesus when the eight days were accomplished for the brit milah of the child, his name was called [*Yeshua*], which was so named of the angel before he was conceived in the womb" (*refer to Matthew 1:20-21*).

Jewish boys received a Hebrew name on the day of circumcision, rather than an English transliteration of a Greek word, or a Greek name.

A Jew is known by his own Hebrew name and that of his father (X son of Y). In that form he is "called up" to the Reading of the Law in the synagogue.

ישוע

Education and Trade

Chapter 4

Jesus ~ Jewish Education and Trade

Avot 5:24, in Jewish tradition had written, "...*at twenty years of age for seeking a livelihood.*"

Did Jesus become involved in seeking a livelihood at the age of twenty years?

That question can't be answered with any certainty from New Testament sources. But we do know the words of the people about Jesus in Mark 6:3, when they said;

> *Is not this the carpenter, the son of Mary, the brother of James, and Joses, and of Juda, and Simon? And are not his sisters here with us? All the local folks were amazed at his teachings and mighty works.*

The King James Version and its Greek manuscript

copies, accurately name 4 brothers and 2 unnamed sisters of Jesus. Yet, some contend that the verse does not actually mean literal "sisters," but may mean cousins. Other scholars have also suggested that Joseph had children of his own by a previous marriage before Mary. Gospel evidence indicates that Joseph and Mary had other children after Jesus was born. This is realized after comparing Mark 6:3 with the verses of Mark 6:33-35.

In one setting when Jesus was teaching, the narrative relates that the mother and brothers are standing without the crowd and calling to Jesus, then Jesus makes that situation an example about his family and the things of God. Jesus said; *"Who is my mother, or my brethren?"* He then looks upon the crowd and says about his listeners:

> *Behold my mother and my brethren. Whosoever shall do the will of God, the same is my brother, and my sister and mother.*

Such analogy would not have worked well, if it were not his immediate family who were calling to him as he taught the crowd.

But, our real point of focus beyond what folks said about him is that they also called Jesus the carpenter, when he was about 30 years of age, and began his public ministry. That biblical statement when combined with the knowledge of Avot 5:24, implies that Jesus had been learning and practicing the carpenter trade for possibly 10 years.

Learning a trade is not a matter involving only one year of experience. His reputation among the people was already- the carpenter. He entered into his "full strength" at 30 years of age when he began to preach and teach as an adult. According to the book of Numbers chapter four, at the same age, Levites began serving in the Temple (see Numbers 4:3, 4:23, 4:30, and Numbers 4:35).

One of several things that Jewish fathers were to teach a son, was a trade or occupation. When reading Matthew 13:55, we learn that the populace assumed that Jesus was the son of Joseph, and knew that Joseph was also known as a carpenter.

The New Testament Greek word is tektwn (*tekton*), and may also mean a skilled trade. That definition is listed as a secondary meaning in some Intermediate Greek English Lexicons, as well as any craftsman. Yes, Jesus knew a trade, as well as his adoptive father, Joseph.

The Talmud emphasizes *"A father is to circumcise his son, teach him Torah, take a wife for him, and teach him a trade."*

The silence of our New Testament sources about Jesus and his youth causes us to question somewhat, and the usual Christian stance is not to assume a matter. Though information is lacking about Jesus in the years between age 12 and age 30, there are Jewish sources which shed light on custom and practices for parents to follow when bringing up children.

We are aware of some Jewish customs and tradition which possibly sheds light on Jesus' childhood and youth. If this rabbinic wisdom was followed, and there is no reason to doubt it wasn't, then we can be assured that at pivotal points of his childhood and youth, basic things were planned for his life.

The Sayings of the Fathers (*Pirkei Avot*), consists of the moral and practical teachings of some 60 sages whose lives spanned nearly 5 centuries. The teachings were compiled in the early third century by Judah ha-Nasi, and reflected a vast number of opinions expressed over centuries in the learning academies, primarily in the land of Israel. He sifted through, evaluated, and edited the oral law, putting it into writing. From his work, the Pirkei Avot is passed down. It contains the wisdom of the great rabbis whose scholarship and humanity shaped the development of Judaism. We have no reason to doubt that this wisdom was put into practice and taught by word of mouth long before it was put into writing.

Let's take a look at some of those "*sayings.*"

> Avot 5:24 *At five years the age is reached for the study of scripture, at ten for the study of the Mishnah, at thirteen for the fulfillment of the commandments, at eighteen for marriage, at twenty for seeking a liveli- hood, at thirty for entering into ones full strength, at forty for understanding, at fifty for counsel, at sixty a man attains old age, at seventy the hoary head, at eighty the gift of special strength, at ninty he bends beneath the weight of years, at a hundred he is as if he were already dead and had passed away from the world.*

Jesus' life was cut off in the midst of his years. He only lived to be approximately 33 years of age, and had entered into his full strength. He didn't marry, and later I will discuss that with our readers and give some possible reasons why. ***Did the parents of Jesus follow that pattern, as outlined by Judah son of Tema?***

Jesus was from an orthodox family, and we are inclined to admit that the possibility of Jesus learning scripture at 5 years of age was not unreasonable at all. Knowing the Hebrew Bible was part of the command of God for all offspring of Israel, as recorded in Deuteronomy 6:7

> *You shall teach them diligently unto your children and talk of them when you sit in your house, and when you walk by the way, and when you lie down, and when you rise up.*

Surely, Yosef and Miriam (Joseph and Mary) spent much time with Jesus teaching, repeating, and talking scripture.

Sources assert that the first biblical verse taught by a father to his son is in Deuteronomy 6:4, called the *shema*. The translation would say:

> *Hear O Israel, The Lord is our God, the Lord is One.*

It's called the *shema*, because of the first Hebrew word, *which means hear.*

We might say the shema is a confession of faith, and focuses on the revelation to Israel, that

Elohim is One (*Elohim echad*). The verse is generally recited twice a day, once in the morning and once in the evening.

The child would say these words:

"Shema Yisrael, Hashem Eloheynu Hashem echad."

Imagine the child Jesus reciting the verse twice a day.

For my own personal satisfaction, I have learned and memorized the same verse, even though I'm a Gentile. It's a powerful verse.

Prior to his teens, when Jesus was at the age of 12 years as written in Luke 2:42-52, mention is made of his behavior, in that, when his parents decided to go home from Temple, Jesus was still talking and discussing matters with the "teachers." The parents had supposed that Jesus was in the company of people heading home only to eventually realize he was missing. Joseph and Mary were stressed out, and returned to the Temple and found him after three days. They scolded him and he responded saying,

Know you not that I must be about my Fathers business.

"Nevertheless, Jesus went down with them, - and was SUBJECT unto them (his parents)."

Such reverent behavior by a 12 year old boy is commendable and reflects discipline and ethics in action. But, it didn't just happen. It was behavior by choice and not by chance. It was surely because of Torah influence and parental example.

Other New Testament verses exist which can be used to show an example of childhood parenting of a Jewish child. In one case the father was a Greek, but the mother was a Jewess.

The verse in consideration is located in 2Timothy 3:14-15, and relates to Timothy (see Acts 16:1).

According to Apostle Paul's own words or writings, as a child Timothy was well taught and knew scriptures from the Hebrew tradition. In spite of the fact Timothy's earthly father was a Gentile, he (Timothy) still knew the Holy Scriptures. *How did he learn them?* Of course; his mother had taught him.

In 2Timothy 1:5, Paul calls to remembrance the unfeigned faith indwelling Timothy, his grandmother Lois, and mother Eunice. Some details are lacking about these 2 women, but our New Testament source indicates their knowledge of faith gained by knowing the scriptures, had been passed along to timothy. That faith was beneficial to Timothy, and produced trust in the Lord, rather than a *"legalist attitude."* It needs also to be stressed that such *"faith"* came from what is called the Old Testament, because the New Testament had not yet been written.

Some Christians may think that any verses from the Old Testament or law section of their Bible are no longer valid and produce no true faith. *Wasn't it a Hebrew prophet named Habbakuk who wrote: "the just shall live by his faith?"*

Acts 16:3 reveals that Paul knew the value of keeping the laws of God, and took his young Christian convert and had him circumcised. This made it possible for the young man to travel among Jews with Paul in the ministry, thus lessening animosity. They knew Timothy's father was Greek, as well they knew or had heard of Paul's conversion to the message of Jesus. The resentment was there and Paul wasn't willing to demean God's laws about the Temple. No need to provoke or stir up agitation more than minimum.

This example about Timothy suggests that Paul's words about my own son in the faith (1Timothy 1:2), reflect back on Timothy's father who failed to have the Jewish boy circumcised. That circumcision was supposed to be arranged by his father, who in tradition was responsible. Paul had assumed a fatherly duty for a Jewish mother's son. This knowledge about that incident sheds insight on situations during and near the "time of Jesus."

The actions and traditions of Jewish mothers and grandmothers, and responsibility of fathers, indicates how things were impressed upon the minds of sons and daughters, about the faith of the forefathers.

The only Bible read in the years of the life of mothers and grandmothers during those years before the arrival of Jesus, was the Hebrew Bible, or the Septuagint, a Greek translation from the Hebrew.

The New Testament was not yet written, so now we can actually understand what Paul meant when he wrote or spoke of scripture. Add to that information the fact that Jewish culture and oral traditions never seem to change in the Orthodox community. Even over periods of hundreds and hundreds of years.

We gain a picture of how Jesus lived and learned as a youth. We also know somewhat of how Jesus looked or his personal appearance.

Comparative analysis sometimes can help us gain the actual likelihood by example among contemporaries, when coupled with some biblical evidence.

What did Jesus look like at twelve or thirty? Was he clean shaven like some Romans or Greeks?

The scriptures have the answer in Leviticus 19:27. Those verses give details about the Jewish male, which according to ultra orthodox Jewish tradition is not given a haircut until he is three years of age.

But then the child is introduced to Leviticus 19:27, which says:

> *Ye shall not round the corners of your head; neither shalt thou mar the corners of thy beard.*

This is explained as not *"cutting the sideburns"* (*peyot*).

The Hebrew Bible covers every aspect of Jewish life, and human relations. Even ethics, morality, governmental responsibility, or any matter of importance.

Now we know why Jesus and Orthodox Jews had those long dangling sideburns with beards.

It's never difficult to know, to determine, if the Jew you meet is Orthodox, Conservative, or Reform. Just imagine who the literalist could be based on peyot, and bingo, you know which is the strictest as to the interpretations of the writings of Moses.

Yeah, imagine Jesus at 30 years of age, with those long dangling sideburns.

Apostle Peter wrote the following of Jesus in 1Peter 2:22; *"Who did no sin, neither was guile found in his mouth."*

Sin is transgression of Gods law, and Apostle Peter said that Jesus did not sin.

"HEBREWS DRINK FROM
THE SPRING,

THE GREEKS
FROM THE STREAM THAT
FLOWS FROM IT,

AND THE LATINS
FROM A DOWNSTREAM POOL."

(Martin Luther)

ישוע

and Marriage

Chapter 5

Jesus and Marriage

Since marriage is normal and holy in Jewish thought, **why then, was Jesus never married?** Good question!

We don't have sufficient wisdom to fully explain why he didn't marry, nor do we have any clear cut Bible verses to inform us. But, we do have some biblical information for well based speculation, based on instruction given by the Lord to one of His prophets in regard to "taking a wife."

The reading of Jeremiah 16:1-13, mentions that the Lord had forbidden that prophet to marry. Jeremiah was to devote himself to the task of preaching Gods coming judgment upon Judah and Jerusalem because of unrepentant sins.

In the Divine call upon his life to prophetic ministry as given in the first chapter of his book saying;

Before I formed thee in the belly I knew thee; and before thou camest forth out of the womb I sanctified thee, and I ordained thee a prophet unto the nations.

God's "calling" and purpose for Jeremiah was much more important than his marriage status, for the destinies of Judah and Jerusalem were involved.

Some teachers have asserted that the negative nature of such a ministry as Jeremiah's could only produce severe unhappiness for a wife as well as her mate. The prophet's life and about 41 years of ministry were also going to be burdened with knowledge that the Lord would soon bring an end to Jerusalem and cause the casting away of the covenant people.

Remember what the Lord had told the prophet in Jeremiah 1:10; *"root out, and pull down, and to destroy, and to throw down, to build, and to plant."*

Jeremiah's ministry caused him much sorrow, and he became known among his people as the weeping prophet.

The Lord had told Jeremiah in 16:2,

You shall not take a wife; neither

shall you have sons or daughters in this place.

We do speculate that God foresaw what suffering and sorrow would come to a wife and children, and spared some suffering by commanding Jeremiah not to marry. He too being a prophet was aware of the tragedies, the grief of many deaths, and the terrible impact of sword, and famine upon his people. He rather mourned for all the great evils that would befall his people, for the Lord had said He would take away His peace from this people, even lovingkindness and mercies.

In that situation and because of all the judgment and tragedy to come, marriage seemed out of the question.

Similar reasons may be why Jesus did not marry. Various verses in the Christian Bible show that Jesus had a keen sense of destiny involving much suffering and sorrow. He mentioned suffering at the hands of the Gentiles (Mark 9:31 and Mark 10:33-34), as well as rejection by the scribes and elders, who would eventually betray him over to the Gentiles. He foresaw what was to come.

He must have known early on and long before his 18th year of age (*Pirkei Avot*), the suggested age for males to marry. Near the moment of his death on the cross by Roman crucifixion, he saw fit to commend his mother into the care of John the Beloved (John 19:26-27), rather than the care of his four literal "brothers."

Imagine how sensitive he was, and imagine if he was a married man. What a complicated scenario! The school leaving age in the scheme of a Jewish child's education was suggested to be 20, but marriage was suggested to be at 18 (Avot 5:24).

Sources say that during the first years of marriage, the student-husband usually lived with, and was supported by his wife's parents. Imagine, if Jesus had not been single.

In Genesis 1:28 it was recorded that God said unto mankind, *p-ru urvu umil-u et ha-aretz*, Be fruitful and multiply and fill the earth. In Hebrew teaching this is the first of 613 commandments, in the Torah.

That positive command about procreation becomes a point of contention about Jesus among Jews, since Jesus did not take a wife. The case is made for an argument that Jesus did not fulfill all the obligations of the Torah. But, neither did Jeremiah, who was despised somewhat by Jews for all his negative and judgmental words.

Later in history and today, Jeremiah is deemed by good Jews as one of the greatest of the prophets. But Jeremiah did not marry or take a wife after the Lord God told him not to do so.

In Judaism marriage is holy and a good thing and marriages are usually arranged on a Tuesday.

Why do they arrange a marriage on that day? Simply because scripture says on the third creative day, that God saw that it was good. The terms are written twice on that particular day. How is that for literally taking the scriptures as final?

A wife was also considered good, because of the Hebrew wording of Genesis 2:18, which wrote:

eh-esh lo eyzer k-negdo.

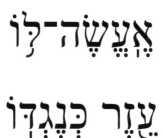

אֶעֱשֶׂה־לּוֹ

עֵזֶר כְּנֶגְדּוֹ

"I will make him a helper for him."

Some commentary on the verse says: *"Man's mate is either his helper if he is fortunate, or against him if he is not."*

That logic is based on the meaning of the Hebrew word which was rendered "helpmeet" in our King James Version Bible. The root term means contradict, oppose, or be against.

It's very interesting to say the least, that God's comment, I will make, is in direct contrast to the plural form "Let us make."

The sages say that the plural sense (let us), is explained by the fact that man, woman, and God are three involved in the procreative or reproductive process. This appears to be borne out by Genesis 5:3, saying, Adam-begat a son in his own likeness, after his image; and called his name Seth.

The first man Adam had neither human father nor earthly mother, yet Luke 3:38 calls him the son of God.

The angel Gabriel announced that Jesus would be called "son of the highest" (Luke 1:32). New Testament writings assert that Jesus is the second Adam in First Corinthians.

The second Adam took no wife and begat no literal children, while the first Adam took a wife and begat both sons and daughters. The second Adam was born of a woman, while the first Adam was not born with human parents.

Although Jesus never married or begat literal sons and daughters... New Testament authors allude that every person who comes to God because of Jesus are called "sons of God." (John 1:12-13, Hebrews 2:10, 1John 3:1-2).

יֵשׁוּעַ

as Rabbi

רַבִּי

Chapter 6

Jesus ~ as Rabbi רַבִּי

Was Jesus actually an ordained rabbi?
According to information gleaned from all Gospel
accounts, we must admit the answer is no. But
internal sources indicate that he was called "rabbi"
in various narrative situations.

Any Exhaustive Concordance of the Bible
(K.J.V.) shows that the Greek Testament term
"rabbi" was translated 9 times into the English word
"master" in the four Gospels. In another 7 gospel
verses, English translators actually wrote the word
"rabbi" where the Hebrew "rabbi" appeared in the
gospels. Some scholars have suggested that Jesus
was an itinerant rabbi; and that kind of fits the
description of one who travels from place to place
preaching or teaching the word of God. That
description fits Jesus and numerous others
mentioned in the New Testament writings.

The appearance of 16 examples of the Hebrew

term "Rabbi" during conversations within New Testament Greek Gospels is revealing.

It was not unusual in those days, for honor to be bestowed upon certain persons who travelled and taught the word of God, the honorable title of Rabbi. We find that example in the case of John the Baptist in John 3:26;

> *And they came unto John, and said unto him, Rabbi, he that was with thee beyond Jordan, to whom thou bearest witness, behold, the same baptizeth, and all (men) come unto him.*

We have never been told by our leaders, that John the Baptizer was known by the term "rabbi" in both the Greek and English Gospels. Revealing indeed!

Far back in Hebrew Bible times, the term "Rav" had been used to show honor to officials as well. It is noted with names like Rab-Mag, Rab-Saris, and Rab-Shakeh, as found in verses like Jeremiah 39:3, and 2Kings 18:17. Those incidents were references to Babylonian and Assyrian princes. Authority figures were given a measure of respect similar to that shown to scholars or teachers.

The Hebrew term "rav" means much, many, or more. When the suffix is added to "rav," it became rabbi, and relates to more than me, which of course refers to one who is more than me; my teacher.

Throughout the four Gospels, the English translation term "master" has a tendency to cloud the truth about the Greek manuscript use of the term

Rabbi

רַבִּי

The Greek New Testament Gospel narratives likewise indicate that the term "teacher" (dida-skale), is interchangeable with "rabbi," as found in John 1:38.

These examples do not relate to actual ordination which in Hebrew is called semikhah (laying on of hands). But they reflect the acceptance by the people of God, of authority figures, and leaders who were given sorts of honor.

There is biblical evidence in Numbers 27:18 and Numbers 27:23, where Moses laid hands on Joshua, thus establishing his successor. That transfer of authority is similar to the handing down of Torah teachings, as mentioned in Avot 1:1:

"Moses received the Torah on

Sinai, and handed it down to Joshua; and Joshua to the elders, the elders to the prophets; and the prophets handed it down to the men of the great assembly."

The transmission of truth into Jewish hands is also reflected in the message of Numbers 11:24-25,

When Moses and the Lord ordained 70 elders who assisted in developing the nation of Israel. And Moses went out...and gathered the seventy men of the elders of Israel...And the Lord came down in a cloud... and took of the Spirit that was upon him...and gave it unto the seventy elders.

In this case the authority transfer and continuation of teaching, was given by the Lord, and according to Jewish tradition, the Talmud mentions that the seventy elders later ordained others, continuing down to The Second Temple period. The Spirit that was upon Moses was given also unto the elders of Israel, resting upon them, and they prophesied "without ceasing" round about the Tabernacle.

Likewise, two others in the camp named Eldad and Medad prophesied constantly. This shows that others even beyond selection process of the leaders, may be used of God to bring the word of the Lord to His people, and are to be honored as the bearers of His message.

Jesus travelled throughout Galilee preaching and teaching about the Kingdom of God (heaven), and was honored by his hearers with the title "rabbi." He also appointed and authorized 82 of his chosen students to proclaim his good news that the kingdom of God was at hand.

The honor of "rabbi" was bestowed him by thousands who listened and were helped and healed by his message. *Not bad for a rabbi, who wasn't really a rabbi by semikhah standards.*

A verse in Acts 10:38 gives specific information about Jesus and his authority: " God anointed Jesus of Nazareth with the Holy Ghost and with power: who went about doing good, and healing all that were oppressed of the devil; for God was with him." The anointing of the Holy Spirit with power was his authorization, and his good works were vindication.

In the absence of semikhah, God had issued a message from heaven at Jesus' baptism in Matthew 3:16-17.

This is known in Judaism as

a bat kol

בַּת קוֹל

or daughter of a voice.

"This is my beloved son, in whom I am well pleased."

A voice from heaven (bat kol), was understood as a supernatural method of communicating God's will to men-- after the Hebrew prophets had come to an end.

If Jesus was chosen of God, anointed of God, declared pleasing to God, and proved to be a doer of mighty works and deeds; then why should he not be honored by men who recognize that from his mouth come the words of God and Moses?

Being authorized by the Lord to teach, is honorable, and is as important as a title.

ANCIENT HEBREW WISDOM

FALSEHOOD IS COMMON,
TRUTH UNCOMMON

(Shab. 104^a; D. 641).

ישוע

Kingdom Message

Chapter 7

Jesus' Kingdom Message

There are those who think that the kingdom of God and the kingdom of heaven are two different things; but I wish to present what I consider is accurate presentation on the subject. The Gospels of Matthew, Mark, Luke, and John, contain many things which Jesus spoke and taught, and one of the most recurrent subjects in the four Gospels, is the kingdom of God or kingdom of heaven.

Studious persons know from examination of the Greek manuscript copies, that Jesus favorite self imposed name or term, was the Son of man and one of his favorite themes was the Kingdom of God or Kingdom of heaven. An explanation about evasive synonyms with an example of such based on interpretation of a bible verse, could shed light on the subject kingdom of God or kingdom of heaven.

We should understand that the Jewish mindset of the people of Jesus' time was inclined to avoid overmuch usage of a Divine name, both in speech and in writing. This was the result of sacred respect, and in connection with an interpretation of Exodus 20:7 (K.J.V.) which stated: *"Thou shall not take the Name of the LORD thy GOD in vain."*

Gentile Christians are inclined to think that the verse means no cussing involving the Divine names. But when one recognizes that Hebrew is a holy language/tongue, and there were no cuss words in ancient and biblical Hebrew, it becomes easier to comprehend what was originally meant.

Scholars and Orthodox Jews developed a reverential respect for the primary and secondary names of God, and hoped to do nothing that would bring shame or disgrace to God or His teachings.

Naturally, people are not supposed to fill their mouths with foul, crude, and degrading speech, but to properly interpret what scripture has meant in many situations, we must examine our Hebrew roots and culture.

What was called evasive synonyms, were developed to avoid disrespect for the Divine name, and to avoid common usage. Terms like *Adonai* and *Hashem* became the substitutes in prayer, conversation, and literature.

They became the normal way to talk about...

יהוה

(YHVH) and

אלהים

(ELOHIM)

throughout Judaism, and is traced back many generations.

Knowing this bit of information makes it quicker to grasp that the word "heaven" is an evasive synonym for "God." As seen here: the kingdom of heaven, or the kingdom of God.

Matter of fact, in Jewish theology, the kingdom of heaven and the Kingdom of God are the same, but as in Christian theology, subtle nuances are involved.

A subject often discussed by Jesus in the Gospels was the kingdom of God/heaven. He used the term lots of times in his parables and stories. In five (5) verses in Matthew's Gospel, he mentions kingdom of God, and in thirty one (31) verses he speaks of the kingdom of heaven. So, thirty six (36)

Matthew verses have Jesus talking on that subject (verse locations given below).

In Mark's Gospel, the term kingdom of God is located in fifteen verses (15), but the phrase kingdom of heaven is not found in Marks Gospel. The Gospel of Luke shows the term kingdom of God in thirty one verses (31), yet, the phrase kingdom of heaven is not found there either.

Lastly, the Gospel of John reveals that kingdom of God is written in two verses (2). But, the terminology kingdom of heaven isn't written in John's Gospel.

We are uncertain as to why the gospel authors of Mark, Luke, and John chose NOT to use the evasive synonym heaven for the word God (*Greek-ouranoV =ouranos*), but do think it important to show the frequency of the forms used. The combined number of verses relating to the Kingdom of God or heaven in the four Gospels is about 84 mentions. It seems that one of Jesus' favorite subjects is the kingdom of God or kingdom of heaven.

During his earthly sojourn, Jesus and his followers were familiar with the Roman Empire and its rule, and it's certain that Israel and the Jews wanted freedom from the harsh and tyrannical rule of the Romans. His parables about the kingdom of

God brought hope and enlightenment to listeners who were being oppressed by Roman rule.

From the Daniel visionary scenario, in the book of Daniel, we have read that one aspect of "kingdom" is linked to the word empire.

Daniel's writings foretold of the rise and fall of empires and kingdoms, beginning with Babylon, Medo Persian, Greece, Rome, and the 10 nation combination.

But, all were finally crushed by the Stone which became a mountain and filled the whole earth. (Daniel 2:35).

Daniel 2:44 relates that

> *"The God of heaven in the days of those kings will set up a kingdom which shall never be destroyed ... and it shall stand for ever."*

Then in Daniel 7:13,

> *"One like a Son of Man, came with the clouds of heaven, and came to the Ancient of Days.*

Verse 14 mentions;

> *"There was given him dominion, glory, and a kingdom, that all people, nations, and languages, should serve him."*

That one, like a son of man is the choice of God to rule all nations for ever, after the kingdoms of this world are brought to nought. This is the only time in the entire Bible that the Aramaic term for son of man occurs.

(*bar enosh*)

Best I have found, is that the Aramaic term (bar enosh), although occurring only once in the K.J. Version Bible, was also used in other non biblical writings of Aramaic origin and denoted humanity in many cases.

That interpretation does not apply in the Daniel 7:13 passage, where it is found. The reason is, in that particular example, he alone was given dominion, glory, and a kingdom that all people, nations, and languages should serve him. That Son of Man is to rule the kingdom of God in Daniels writings, and his kingdom shall never be destroyed.

Elsewhere the terms son of man appear from the Hebrew.

בֶּן אָדָם

(*ben adam*)

Since Daniel 7:13 is written in Aramaic, it becomes the only Bible passage where this very different term appears. The Ezekiel son of man verses do not contain the very special term, which is reserved for only the one designated by the Ancient of Days as future world ruler of the kingdom of God on this earth.

It also is known by other verses that Jesus' favorite term about himself, is the Son of man. That term is representative of the most supernatural king or leader in all human history, since he alone is given final and everlasting dominion.

In Matthew's gospel Jesus names himself as the Son of man (Matt. 16:13), and asks Peter; whom do men say that I the Son of man am ? Although Jesus identifies himself as the Son of man, Peter eventually names him as the messiah (Greek-Christ), based on Peter's personal revelation from the Father. The frequency of use of the phrase regarding Jesus by himself in the 4 gospels leaves little doubt as to whom Jesus wished to identify with his person.

I have found 31 Matthew verses with that self used term, 14 Mark verses, Luke wrote 25 verses, and John used the term Son of man in 11 verses. Sum total= 81 gospel verses using Son of man. No doubt that term was Jesus' favorite self identifying phrase.

So, according to Christian verses, Jesus is both Messiah (Greek/Christ), and Son of man. Scholars know that Jesus rarely made self reference as "Christ" but always promoted himself as Son of man.

In the evolving of Christianity other Christian authors make much reference to him as "Christ"; but hardly ever did Jesus make that claim. Others made it for him. He knew who he was and didn't require human approval.

For the purposes of study of the kingdom of God or heaven, the prophetic and futuristic aspect of the kingdom in this world, must entail the phrase Son of man, which connects mightily with a future world ruler, who under God will rule in His behalf.

We should also consider the present aspect of the kingdom. The literal crowning and enthroning of the Son of man, is to be futuristic, when it will no longer be perfume anointing for his burial, or a thorn crown of suffering. It will be with literal holy oil as designated by Moses, and hinted at by the Psalmist who wrote: *"Yet have I *set My king, upon My holy hill of Zion" /Tzion* (Psalm 2:6).

A better translation would use the words *anointed my king.* This is prophetic. It's also literal. No anointing of an Israelite or Jewish king have I found in history to have taken place on the hill called Tzion.

In spite of the fact that King David was 3 times literally anointed with holy oil, being anointed at Bethlehem and Hebron. The Hebrew writing looked thus:

$$\text{וַאֲנִי נָסַכְתִּי מַלְכִּי}$$

$$\text{עַל־צִיּוֹן הַר־קָדְשִׁי,}$$

The Hebrew biblical term *"nasachti,"* could also be translated "I anoint" *(source-a Hebrew pocket dictionary under "nasakh").*

The angel Gabriel in Luke 1:32, foretold that the Lord God shall give unto him (Jesus), the throne of his father David. He also foretold that Jesus shall reign over the house of Jacob for ever; and of his kingdom there shall be no end (Luke 1:33).

These verses, no matter how we may spiritualize them, are to be taken literally, and indicate WHO will be delegated as heir of David's throne for ever. Thus, the kingdom had a present meaning as well as a future aspect. But, as yet Jesus has never set on David's throne, or received a literal non spiritual kingdom.

Jesus spoke of the Son of man coming in power and glory, and with the holy angels; and of a time when he would be on the throne of glory (Matthew 25:31). All these things are futuristic and have not yet happened.

It is quite important to understand when we speak of the kingdom of God or kingdom of heaven, exactly which aspect we are alluding, present or future.

In the Jewish tradition, when a boy or girl becomes of age to take upon themselves the responsibilities of adulthood (*bar mitzvah-bat mitzvah*), the sages have said that at such a moment they take upon themselves the yoke of the kingdom of heaven or...

קבלת עול מלכות שמים

Those were the actual Hebrew words.

Those words show that Jewish children at
certain age, accept the yoke of the kingdom of God ,
which involves submitting to Gods teachings-
becoming a subject of the kingdom. The notion of
Gods kingdom, or the kingdom of heaven was
immediate in that sense, because God was "King"
over ones life (See Psalm 5:2 and Psalm 10:16).

The son of man was destined to become a
"king," according to prophecies of Daniel, and Jesus
viewed himself as the fulfillment of that and many
other prophecies. Notice the wording of some of his
son of man prophecies:

> Matthew 8:20, *"the Son of man
> hath not where to lay his head"*

> Matthew 9:6, *"the Son of man hath
> power on earth to forgive sins"*

> Matthew 12:8, *"the Son of man is
> Lord even of the sabbath day"*

> Matthew 12:40, *"the Son of man be
> three days and three nights in the
> (earth)"*

> Matthew 13:37, *"He that soweth
> the good seed is the Son of man"*

Matthew 13:41, *"The Son of man shall send forth his angels, and they shall gather out of his kingdom all things that offend"*

Matthew 16:13, *"Whom do men say that I the Son of man am?"*

Matthew 16:27, *"For the Son of man shall come in the glory of his Father"*

Matthew 16:28, *"Till they see the Son of man coming in his kingdom"*

Matthew 17:9, *"Tell the vision to no man till the Son of man be risen again from the dead"*

Matthew 17:12, *"Likewise shall also the Son of man suffer of them?"*

Matthew 17:22, *"The Son of man shall be betrayed into the hands of men"*

Matthew 18:11, *"For the Son of man is come to save that which was lost"*

Matthew 19:28, *"The Son of man shall sit in the throne of his glory, ye also shall sit"*

Matthew 20:18, *"The Son of man shall be betrayed unto the chief priests"*

Matthew 24:27, *"As the lightning cometh out of the East, and shineth even unto the West; so shall also the coming of the Son of man be"*

Matthew 24:30, *"Then shall appear the sign of the Son of man in heaven; .and they shall see the Son of man coming in the clouds of heaven"*

Matthew 24:37, *"As the days of Noe were, so shall also the coming of the Son of man be"*

Matthew 24:44, *"For in such an hour as you think not, the Son of man cometh"*

Matthew 25:13, *"Watch therefore, for you know neither the day nor the hour wherein the Son of man cometh"*

Matthew 25:31, *"When the Son of man shall come in his glory, and all the holy angels"*

Matthew 26:2, *"After two days- the Son of man is betrayed to be crucified"*

Matthew 26:24, *"The Son of man goeth as it is written of him, but woe unto…"*

Matthew 26:64, *"Ye [shall] see the Son of man sitting on the right hand of power"*

Those are just some of the Matthew verses where the Son of man term appears, and links to kingdom. There are many more examples in Mark, Luke and John. But these are more than enough verses to show that Jesus knew himself scripturally as the Son of man.

These and many more verses substantiate my claim about the Son of man being his favorite self expression. Hardly ever did Jesus claim to be the Christ (Messiah), but in a few passages he did allow that allusion, The term Christ became a more popular development as the church evolved into another gospel about him, rather then the actual gospel he preached in synagogues throughout all Galilee (see Matthew 4:23, Matthew 9:35, Mark 1:14-15, Luke 9:2, and Luke 9:6).

It's almost impossible for people to grasp that Jesus' gospel and his Son of man teachings among the Jewish people, were very different than the death, burial, and resurrection verses which later became standard Christian gospel about Jesus. Nor, can they imagine what gospel of the kingdom that both he and his disciples preached in synagogues of Galilee. Yet when he began speaking in the last year of his ministry about his rejection, sufferings, death and rising, they were bewildered and shocked.

If it was the same gospel, as the earliest form he preached and taught them, why didn't they grasp it? The earliest form of gospel which he preached in Jewish synagogues was about the kingdom of God (at hand).

My studies indicate without doubt that although his chosen disciples (Luke 10=70 and Luke 9:1=12; total 82), preached his gospel throughout synagogues of Galilee in Luke 9:35, and Mark 1:14-15, they knew nothing about his death burial and resurrection gospel at those times.

As was stated in Mark 9:31, the Son of man is delivered into the hands of men, and they shall kill him; and after that he shall rise the third day. But they understood not that saying, and were afraid to ask him. That verse and numerous others show, although he preached a gospel of the kingdom in synagogues, and his disciples likewise, they had no clue as yet about his death burial and resurrection gospel, which developed before his ascension.

The gospel Jesus preached was different than the message God later gave to Paul. The Greek term for gospel in all manuscript cases is the root form *euaggelion* and equates "good news."

The earliest form of the gospel which Jesus and his disciples preached in synagogues was the good news about the nearness of God's reign. It was the gospel of the kingdom which was at hand. "Tell Tzion; YOUR GOD REIGNS."

See Luke 9:2 and Luke 9:6 which reveal that the disciples also preached his synagogue gospel of the kingdom, working healings, exorcisms, and miracles, as they encouraged men to repent of sins.

The gospel about Jesus Christ was regarding his death, burial, and resurrection, and benefits of acceptance. That gospel of salvation which his disciples later preached, was never accepted or heard in Jewish synagogues, and would never have been accepted for a second synagogue proclamation.

A careful study of the Greek manuscript and *Septuagint* terms rendered "gospel" or good news indicate the same root meaning in all the cases I have examined. Thus, we can only wonder why Paul implied a curse on anyone who preached a different or other gospel than what he proclaimed. Of course, a post resurrection gospel is surely what he meant: a gospel other than the one Paul preached as a means of salvation.

We do well however, to recall the words of the Master who said in Matthew 24:14:

> *And, this gospel of the kingdom*
> *shall be preached in all the world*
> *for a witness unto all nations; and*
> *then shall the end come.*

The prophecy preachers in Christian circles never seem to comprehend that the gospel of the kingdom which Jesus preached in Jewish synagogues was the earliest form, and at that time had no aspects of Jesus' death, burial, and resurrection. *Thus, if we want to get technically perfect as prophecy teachers like to do, we had better proclaim that BEFORE the end comes.*

The gospel of the kingdom which Jesus and his disciples preached in synagogues and all of Galilee must be demonstrated and proclaimed as a witness to the entire world.

In regard to the spiritual significance of the kingdom of God, in Luke 17:20, Jesus told some Pharisees that the kingdom of God cometh not with observation, but dwells within you. Yet in that same narrative section, he links a son of man to a coming day of judgment, and a future time when a kingdom will be ruled by the Son of Man.

On the basis of those comments we can easily see a twofold aspect regarding a king and a kingdom. Likewise, various Psalms allude to and mention God as Israel and the world's king, and many prayers in Hebrew liturgy relate that God is king of the universe. Verses indicating His rule are located in Psalm 10:16, 24:8-10, 47:2, 47:7, 89:18, and Psalm 95:3. Thus, in Jesus' thinking, the kingdom had a past, present, and future connotation.

He had also told his followers that they should pray to the Father in this manner,

> *Thy kingdom come Thy will be done in earth as in the heavens.*

Among Jews, the kingdom of God held promise of future rule in this world as well as the world to come. Those terms are represented in Hebrew by terms *Olam ha-zeh* and *Olam ha-bah*, yet greater concern is for this world, than the world to come, because only here can a real difference be made for the good.

In the Jewish Bible, prophecies were given that allude to a reign of the Messiah, and verses indicate that it will come about to a David/Solomon type ruler. His kingship was said to be ever lasting and even the heathen and the earth itself would become his possession (Psalm 2:8).

During the times of Samuel the prophet and Solomon king of Israel, after the nation of Israel had been settled, it had been told that one from the lineage of David, would be established as a ruler "for ever" (1Samuel 13:13). That was God's intent, but King Saul failed to follow God's command, and the kingdom was taken from him by the Lord's decree.

God chose David to become Israel's king and David's lineage, if continuing in faithfulness, would never have the kingdom taken from him as was done to Saul.

The sure mercies of the House of David were a covenant of the Lord, and as if to emphasize the rejection of Saul whom was anointed as Israel's first king, David was three times anointed with holy oil. He is the only person in the Bible to ever have three literal anointings with holy oil. And, in continuation of that covenant and oath made to David, a future son of David was destined to rule for ever.

The tradition of a son of David still prevails today. The anointing of Saul was never intended to serve as a badge of approval for the king; rather it was supposed to be a badge of purpose. Saul had failed to obey the command of the Lord as written in Deuteronomy 25:17-19, in regard to destroying the Amalekites.

God's mercy had departed from the house of Saul as noted in 2Samuel 7:14-15, and the new king/kingdom was settled to the house of David, whom scripture calls God's firstborn, higher than kings of the earth. ...Mainly because David was a man after God's own heart.

Secondly, because scripture named David as God's servant.

עַבְדִּי

avdi
(Psalm 89:20)

When scripture used the terms *"My servant,"* it shows great honor and deep insight into that person's character.

When the Lord speaks of that person with

such endearing terms, it reminds us of the same terms used in those verses mentioned in 2Samuel 7:14;

> *I will be his Father, and he shall be My son.*

The promise was extended to David's lineage insomuch, that righteous kings of that order would be the hope of Israel's continual rule. That was observed in the reigns of Solomon and Hezekiah. One rabbinic opinion actually stated that Hezekiah was the messiah.

After the resurrection of Jesus, and before the coming of the Holy Spirit, the immediate disciples of Jesus were still concerned about the "time" of restoring the kingdom to Israel (Acts 1:6). All the tremendous events that had taken place in the past week, and yet the apostles were concerned about Israel's restoration. How interesting! Jesus did not rebuke or reprove them but merely focused their thinking on matters at hand, matters more pressing than Israel's restoration at the moment.

> *"It is not for you to know the times or the seasons, which the Father hath put in His own power."*

The next verse instructs the chosen ones that they should be focused on receiving the power of the

Holy Spirit which would enable them to testify effectively about the death, burial, and resurrection of Jesus. The spiritual movement of the kingdom in the hearts of mankind would cause the movement to continue to grow as mustard seed in this world. To Jesus, the spreading of the message was more important at that time than Israel's restoration. He knew the Fathers plan, and now they also would know.

Before kingdom can come to earth or to Israel, it must come into the hearts of humans. They must willingly hear and believe the message about God's great love for the cosmos (people). The next commission after having received the baptism with the Holy Spirit was given by Jesus, saying;

> *Ye shall be witnesses unto me both in Jerusalem, and in all Judea, and in Samaria, and unto the uttermost part of the earth* (Acts 1:8)

At this time, the notion of Israel and its role in the plan of God's kingdom, must give way to the furtherance of the message of the death, burial, and resurrection of Jesus unto the ends of the earth. Those who were eyewitness of his majesty must attest to the facts.

*Whatever relationship that has to do
with the restoration of Israel, and world empires,
shall be determined in time by
the Heavenly Father.*

ישוע

and the

Law of Moses

Chapter 8

Jesus and the Law of Moses

What was the attitude of Jesus about the Law of Moses? The answer to that question is easily found when one reads the four Gospels.

The gospel narratives contain many comments showing the position of Jesus, as he interacted with various detractors and supporters of the law. Jesus' personal comments show that he believed in, upheld and practiced the Law of Moses, and encouraged others to do the same. Notice Matthew 5:17-19;

> *Think not that I am come to destroy the law, or the prophets: I am not come to destroy, but to fulfill.*

He desired to correct any possible misconception that people might have about his relationship, toward the teachings of God as given by Moses and the prophets.

Our English translation version uses the terms, *I am not come to destroy, but to fulfill.* In Jewish thought a better translation would be; *I have not come to destroy, but to observe.* Jews practice and observe the law and the prophets, and in that way alone can the law be fulfilled. That is the joy and zeal of every observant Jew: to perform what God has said.

Jesus was not concerned with a futuristic or prophetic notion of fulfilling the law on behalf of others. He was concerned about giving his life as a ransom on behalf of others.

The conversation and the narrative involved breaking, doing, and teaching the law. Notice what he said in that respect:

> *Whosoever therefore shall break one of these least commandments, and shall teach men so, he shall be called the least in the kingdom of heaven: but whosoever shall do and teach them, the same shall be called great in the kingdom of heaven.*

Great people do and teach God's commandments. When one lays on a foundation already laid, he is careful to build with accuracy and diligent to follow the pattern already established. Such wisdom is not only applicable to construction projects, but it also holds true in religious instruction. Jesus knew that Moses teachings were uttered by God unto Moses and the children of Israel.

The "peculiar people" who received God's teachings (Israel), were actually called in Hebrew, *am segulah*, which accurately means "treasured people". It's unfortunate that the word "peculiar" stuck, since nowdays it more or less means an oddity.

The children of God are not odd, but they are a king's treasure, because they revere Him and His word. Jesus upheld the Law of Moses, yet at times it is quite clear that he resented some interpretive teachings presented by certain scribes and Pharisees.

A verse in Deuteronomy 4:2 forbids anyone from adding to or detracting from what Moses had plainly spoken. It seems that certain interpretations which lent themselves to doing that very thing or negating what God had spoken were known by Jesus, and he wasn't impressed by those "additions or detractions." Jesus wasn't happy when the people were burdened down with more than what the Torah had written.

In one situation in Mark 7:13, he claimed that such details were making the word of God of "none effect." He believed the word of God was adequate in substance and detail, and punctuated that belief with a well known Hebrew saying familiar with the people in his day:

lo yod veh lo kotzo shel yod
(not a yud or the thorn of a yud)

which came from Greek into English as one jot or one tittle shall in no wise pass [from the law]. The jot in Greek is reference to the iota, the tiniest letter in the Greek alphabet, but in its Hebrew counterpart the yod (yud), which is the smallest Hebrew alphabet letter, has a tiny decorative down stroke, known as the thorn of a yud.

Observing and keeping the law of God for the Jew, is fulfilling the law, even to the smallest detail when possible.

According to Jesus, observing and practicing the law of God makes an individual "shine" like a light to the world, a city set on a hill

(Matthew 5:14). Such a person's good works would be like

...a lamp on a lampstand shining out so as to glorify the Heavenly Father (Matthew 5:16).

Doing "good works" is the Jewish way, but it's not

considered as the way of salvation, although some Christians have not understood that.

Jews also believe in salvation by grace. They know that they possess or have an "everlasting covenant" with God, and are not stressed about "being saved" (as we call it). That relationship is based on grace and covenant. Even Noah found grace in the sight of the Lord long before a gospel of grace was ever preached, and Noah was not Jewish.

Both Christian and Jew should understand that there are **3 types of grace** or favor shown in the scriptures. The **first** type is *undeserved favor*. The **second** type is *favor shown between humans*, and the **last** type of grace in the Bible is *deserved favor*.

Apostle Paul's letters to the churches with strong arguments against "erring theology," have produced a backlash among modern Christians about the law as conflicted with grace. Readers of those epistles have interpreted the law as something bad.

Perhaps they have forgotten the words of Jesus to the churches in the Revelation 22:12,

> *Behold I come quickly; and my*
> *reward is with me, to give every*

*man according as his work shall
be.*

Likewise, in Revelation 22:14,

> *Blessed are they that do his
> commandments that they may
> have right to the tree of life, and
> may enter in to the gates of the
> city.*

Those verses actually reflect what Jesus believed
and taught about the law of Moses, and within the
Jewish community. Evidence supports the view that
Jews which came to faith in Jesus in the earliest
church, continued to associate and worship with
other Temple and synagogue Jews, until it was no
longer possible because of divisiveness and
persecution (Acts 21:20).

On the other hand, earliest church leaders, all
of which were Jews, rejoiced at the repentance and
faith of Gentile conversions (Acts 15:3). And, after
coming together in council at Jerusalem in Acts
15:6, decided that newly converted Gentiles need
not be circumcised, neither be required to keep the
laws of Moses (Acts 15:5).

In a final analysis, James (Jacob), the last
conference speaker with all the others, concluded
that letters be sent to all the churches, obligating

them to do only three things: no idol worship, 2 no eating of blood with meat, 3 no sexual sins. The Holy Spirit also authorized those things as noted in Acts 15:28-29. Thus, Jews and Gentiles could at least eat and talk together in mutual respect without flaunting the teachings of Moses.

It was also concluded that persons interested in learning more could do as James suggested, saying; Moses of old time hath in every city them that preach him, being read in the synagogues every Sabbath day (Acts 15:21).

Earliest church leaders still continued to hold and maintain highest respect for the law of Moses. The New Testament writings confirm that Gentile believers were told to keep all the moral code of the law, as such instructions were given by Paul and others in epistles to the churches.

It's quite easy to show that all the Ten Commandments are reiterated in the New Testament and instructed for Christians to honor as noted in Romans 8:7, which notes that

> *The carnal mind is enmity against*
> *God: for it is not subject to the*
> *law of God, neither indeed can be.*

ישוע

Versus

the *Scribes*

and *Pharisees*

Chapter 9

Jesus Versus Scribes and Pharisees

Jewish writings indicate that there were seven types of Pharisees in and near the time of Jesus, and are written about in the Talmud. Five types of Pharisees among the group mentioned in the Talmud were hypocrites.

When New Testament readers absorb the narrative in the gospels, it is easy to opine that the Pharisees were all bad persons. It is as usual, however, bad people always make "news," moreso than the good persons. The same things go on in our modern world. If you want to make news, just be extremely vocal and outspoken against a very popular politician or prominent figure and that will usually get the "press" or make news.

In Matthew chapter twenty three Jesus said; *"Woe unto you scribes and Pharisees."*

He spoke seven woes in that chapter against the scribes and pharisees who were present at his meeting (Matthew 23:13, 23:14, 23:15, 23:23, 23:25, 23:27, and Matthew 23:29). He also labeled them "hypocrites."

Such personal and straightforward preaching and teaching seems quite unusual, and would cause many people to be offended. But, Jesus was not a pillow prophet or people pleaser. His message was straight to the point. We must however be careful to not judge all Pharisees badly because of some hypocrites.

What is a Pharisee? The Hebrew root term is parash and is located in a concordance number 6567. It means to separate, disperse. The plural form is p'rushim and comes into English as "Pharisees."

This Jewish group of separatists practiced ritual purity and freedom from defilement, and is mentioned in the Talmud. Only 2 groups of Pharisees, of 5 mentioned, are without criticism; the pharisee who loves God, and the pharisee who fears God.

In the gospels certain pharisees are constantly in conflict with Jesus. Considering what is written in the Talmud and what the Christian Bible relates in dialogue between Jesus and certain pharisees, we are able to get a better picture of what was happening. Friction that exists due to differing religious interpretations is one thing, but when friction exists due to hypocrisy, it turns into relentless force. ...Especially when a fearless teacher starts blasting his detractors with scalding words like "hypocrite" in a public setting. *The same gentle Jesus we Christians envision, was outspoken and critical of hypocrisy and pretentiousness.*

Were all Pharisees hypocrites? No, of course not! We can't rightly condemn every pharisee and scribe, because a very vocal group, is always tangling with an itinerant rabbi. When we condemn good people, it's like an artist painting a delicate part of a picture, while using a very broad brush to do the detailed work. Suffice it to say, that the "in house" observation of some Talmud writers, fits quite well into the narrative about Jesus blasting hypocrites at his meetings. That segment of pharisees who constantly antagonized

Jesus in gospel narratives is not necessarily a matter of anti-Shemitic view shown in a literary device. It's the master's observation about hypocrisy "in house." It would be different if Jesus' detractors were not Jews, but they were all Jews. We who are outside the pale of Judaism must realize that the arguments made by Jesus were a polemic against some Jewish hypocrisy, and not against every pharisee.

Josephus, also shed some insight on the

pharisees in *Antiquities* XIII. X.6, saying;

> *The pharisees have delivered unto the people a great many observances by succession from their fathers which are not written in the law of Moses; and for that reason it is said that the sadducees reject them, and say that we are to esteem those observances to be obligatory which are in the written word, but are not to observe what is derived from the tradition of our forefathers; and concerning those things it is that great disputes have arisen among them.*

In defense of the good pharisee, one scholar wrote:

> *Of all that is said against rabbinic Judaism in the writings of the Church Fathers, there is not a single accusation of hypocrisy levelled against the sages.*

Jesus also spoke on behalf of the observant Scribes and Pharisees who sit in "Moses seat." - All therefore whatsoever they bid you observe, that observe and do...

The distinction is clear enough; Jesus is referring to the hypocritical pharisee when he blurted out; *"but do not ye after their works: for they say, and do not."*

He truly resented those who taught and interpreted Torah, but didn't themselves practice all the addendums they promoted. Just like the old English adage: *Don't do as I do; do as I say.*

Leaders should set examples for their followers and not just "lord" it over them.

All the additions which they promoted and taught seemed to be ones that burdened down the people, for he said about them;

> *They bind heavy burdens and grievous to be borne, and lay them on mens shoulders; but they themselves will not move them with one of their fingers. But all their works they do to be seen of men* (Matthew 23:4-5).

Jesus also denounced some of the scribes who aligned themselves with hypocritical pharisees, and pronounced "woe" upon them as well. I located the word "scribes" about 55 times in the gospels (plural), and in many examples it was mentioned with the word pharisees alongside. –

What is a scribe? In the Greek manuscript copies, it is the word *gram-mat-yooce* (1122), and it means; a writer, secretary, relating to one well versed in the Holy Scriptures; law. Authority seems to have been granted them in a general way by virtue of their occupation, but did not include decisive power.

Some leaders aligned themselves with scribes because of the respect attached to them by the Jewish people due to their knowledge of the law.

Thank God for all the sages who
lived for God and practiced what they preached.
Thank God for every "scribe" instructed
in the Kingdom of Heaven.

ANCIENT HEBREW WISDOM

ACCORDING TO
THE GARDEN
IS THE GARDENER

(Gen. R. ch. lxxx. § 1; D. 456).

ישע

and the

Prayer

Shawl~Fringes

Chapter 10

Jesus and the Prayer Shawl~Fringes

Moses had written and commanded Israel under Gods direction, that every male should have "fringes" (KJV), on the border of his garment.

The English Translation wording is found in Numbers 15:38-40, as follows:

> *Speak unto the children of Israel, and bid them that they make them fringes in the borders of their garments throughout their generations, and that they put upon the fringe of the borders a ribband of blue: And it shall be unto you for a fringe, that you may look upon it, and remember all the commandments of the Lord, and do them.*

The Hebrew Bible term for fringes is *tzitzit* (plural tzitziot). The verses refer to a garment known today as *"tallit katan"* (small prayer shawl), differentiating between the *"tallit gadol,"* which is the larger tallit and used mostly when praying.

The smaller tallit is worn during the day by observant male Jews. Looking on a fringe or tzitzit (some render it tassel), was to be a constant reminder to the Jew, to remember and to do all the Lord's commandments, as given by Moses from God.

A good question is: **Did Jesus wear the tzitzit garment?** Does the Christian Bible provide any information which indicates that Jesus kept or obeyed that teaching? The simple answer to both questions posed is yes. I will provide some verses, but we should first learn some important detail related to the word tzitzit.

The Talmud relates in Nedarim 25a, *the wearing of the tzitzit equals the observance of the whole Torah.* How can that be? Explanation is found in the knowledge that the Hebrew language also has a numerical value for each alphabet letter. The number value of the word tzitzit is 600. Sages then added the number of threads and knots in one of the four corners of the garment, which is 13 (eight threads and five knots), and the sum is 613. This is also the exact number of all the Torah

Commandments. Thus, the Talmudic statement about tzitzit, and Torah commands, equal the same in number value.

In Mark 6:56, an account is given of Jesus and his followers:

> *And whithersoever he entered, into villages or city or country, they laid the sick in the streets, and besought him that they might touch if it were but the border of his garment: and as many as touched it were made whole.*

Notice the terms "border of his garment." Then we should examine an exhaustive concordance of the Bible, under the italicized number 2899, for a link to the Greek word rendered border. The word is "kras'pedon." The definitions are listed as; fringe or tassel.

Similar gatherings and events are mentioned in the Gospels (see Matthew 9:20-21, Matthew 14:36, and Mark 5:27-28). In each case the separate gospel authors used the same root term "*kras'pedon.*" How can we doubt that this was simply the fringe or tzitzit? Jesus was wearing the fringed garment, and the people were crowded around him, pressing and surging forward to touch it.

In the process, folks were being made well and healed. More evidence exists beyond the gospel verses. The translation word used in the Septuagint Greek, that is rendered from the Hebrew text in Numbers 15:38-40, and refer to tzitzit, is the same as used in Christian Greek Testament copies.

The word is *"kras'peda."* Keep in mind that the Five Torah books are reported to have been translated around the date 247-288 B.C.E., for Jews of Alexandria, who possibly had lost the use of their mother tongue.

In Jesus' early ministry, many people sought healing from him. Some trusted any word he might say to them. Others wanted him or his disciples to lay hands on them and anoint and pray.

But in numerous gospel narratives, and perhaps because of huge crowds, they sought only to touch the hem of his garment, and as many as touched "it," were made whole.

Heaven rewarded the faith of those
who reached and touched.

FIFTY [ZUZ] WHICH PRODUCE [INCREASE] ARE BETTER THAN A HUNDRED WHICH DO NOT

(j. Peah viii. 8; D. 296).

ישוע

Miracles, Wonders

and Mass Healing

In the Gospels

Chapter 11

Jesus ~ Miracles, Wonders & Mass Healing in the Gospels

Matthew 11:20, mentions that Jesus began to reproach the cities wherein most of his "mighty works" were done. The next verse (v.21), lists Chorazin and Bethsaida, as being upbraided by him, because they had witnessed so many "mighty works," yet had not repented. Afterward, in Matthew 11:23, Jesus mentions another city that had witnessed so many of God's mighty works under his ministry.

And thou, Capernaum, which art exalted unto heaven, shall be brought down to hades: for if the mighty works which have been done in thee, had been done in Sodom, it would have remained until this day.

Jesus named 3 cities that saw and witnessed many "mighty works;" Chorazin, Bethsaida, and Capernaum. The Greek term associated with all these examples where the English renders "mighty works," *is doo'-na-mis*, Greek Conc. # 1411). It's used also in Matthew 13:54-58, which informs us of limitations upon Jesus' ministry, in his own region, and because of family familiarity. The 58th verse says:

> *And he did not many mighty works there because of their unbelief.*

Doubts can certainly hinder some "mighty works." I recall a verse found in Psalms 78:41 (K.J. Version):

> *Yea, they turned back and tempted God, and limited the Holy One of Israel.*

Israel had provoked God and grieved Him in the wilderness, and thereby had placed limitations upon themselves and God's power. Psalm 78:32 gives us insight to the "limitation":

> *"For all this they sinned still, and believed not for His wonderous works."*

The wording, believed not, and unbelief, are the very same in meaning.

However, they were many other instances without limitation reported by the Gospels. Notice, Luke 9:43:

> *And they were all amazed at the mighty power of God, but while they wondered every one at all things which Jesus did, he said unto his disciples*

Then again in Luke 19:37,

> *When all the people saw him descending Mount Olivet; they exclaimed with loud voices: Praise God ...for all the mighty works that they had seen...*

The two disciples on the road to Emmaus sum up the reputation of Jesus among the people...

Luke 24:19 states:

> *Concerning Jesus of Nazareth, which was a prophet mighty in*

*deed and word before God and all
the people....*

Mark 9:39, is also interesting, for in that verse the word "miracle" is rendered by K.J. Version translators, from the same Greek word doo'-na-mis, which in those other examples was rendered "mighty works."

It's found again in Acts 2:22, where Peter uses it of Jesus, saying:

> *Ye men of Israel, hear these words; Jesus of Nazareth, a man approved of God among you by miracles and wonders, and signs, which God did by him in the midst of you...*

We are unable to read the Gospels, without being impressed over and over by the mighty works of God, when Jesus healed, delivered, and exorcised demons from the people.

Peter used **three words** to express the demonstration of God's mighty power. 1. *dunamis,* 2. *teras,* 3. *seimion.* In order as shown, miracle, wonder, and sign.

In Rabbinic thought, that God performed miracles was never questioned, but their purpose was to 'sanctify His great Name in the world.' In addressing the people of Israel, God is accredited with these words:

> *"All the miracles and mighty acts which I have performed for you, were not with the object that you should give me a reward, but that you should honor Me like dutiful children and call Me your Father."*

Gospel narratives also use the term "healing" in some King James Version examples. Those verses reveal an abundance of cures taking place during Jesus' ministry. Matthew 4:23 is one case:

> *And Jesus went about all Galilee, teaching in their synagogues, and preaching the gospel of the kingdom, and healing all manner of sickness and all manner of disease among the people.*

Matthew 9:35, Luke 9:6, and Luke 9:11, are all verses that also use the word healing/ed. Our Greek source is *ther- ap -yoo' -o, # 2323). From it we have evolved an English word similar in meaning: therapy.*

The Hebrew bible contains instances where God declares to "am Yisrael" (people of Israel); *I am the Lord healing you* (Exodus 15:26). The descriptive Divine name there is Yehovah Rophekha. But, what is simply said there in one of the two Hebrew phrases is: HEALING YOU. Thus, Yehovah Rapha is not technically accurate since the Hebrew suffix calls for "you." An accurate translation would be: *For I am Yehovah your Healer* (note, I use the hybrid form Yehovah, rather than the 4 letter Tetragrammaton).

To assert and invoke the Divine name without the inclusive term "YOU," falls short of scriptural completion. God wanted to heal, not only the bitter waters of Marah, but He desired to heal "am Yisrael," and gave specific conditional promises which would remove diseases from them, diseases that had been experienced by Israel's enemies.

Other verses indicate the same. Look at Exodus 23:25:

> *And you shall serve the Lord your God, and He shall bless thy bread, and thy water; and I will take sickness away from the midst of thee.*

The concern of the Lord for Israel's well being in the harsh desert climate, and their sojourning is expressed so nicely in Deuteronomy 8:4:

> *Thy raiment waxed not old upon thee, neither did thy foot swell, these forty years.*

The God of Avraham, the God of Yitzhak, and the God of Yaakov, has always provided for His children, even in hard times. *Is not His name also Yehovah Yireh (Jehovah Jireh)?* Yehovah will see [to it/provide].

King David, in Psalms 103:3, recognized the benefits of the Lord and stated the following:

> *...who forgiveth all thine iniquities; who healeth all thy diseases...*

Forgiveness and healing were not just invented at the cross of Golgotha. God has been forgiving and healing people since the earliest of times. Remember in Genesis 20:17, when Avraham prayed for Avimelech, after the man restored his wife? The verse says:

*So Avraham prayed unto God:
and God healed Avimelech, and
his wife, and his maidservants;
and they bare [children].*

That is the first time in the English Bible version, where a healing takes place as a direct result of prayer, and the word "healed" appears.

Gospel narratives abound with reports of healings and miracles, which happened for people during the teaching and ministry of Jesus. But, can we rely on the stories, as reported to us, or are they just exaggerations or rumors reported by Gospel authors?

We prefer to believe that the Gospel authors are simply revealing what they saw and heard, as they related the amazing things which they witnessed (See Luke 1:1-2 and Acts 1:1). Notice John 21:24-25,

> *This is the disciple which testifieth
> of these things, and wrote these
> things: and we know that his
> testimony is true. And there are
> also many other things which
> Jesus did, the which if they should
> be written everyone, I suppose*

that even the world itself could not contain the scrolls that should be written. Amen.

We find it difficult to dispute what claimed "eyewitnesses," have declared, since we were not there, and since John introduced the "amen," thus attesting to the veracity and authenticity of events which the disciples witnessed.

Imagine; a person so inspired by what he saw and heard of teachings, signs, wonders and miracles that he thought many many more scrolls should be written. Even enough to fill the world... Impressive indeed, enough so as to promote such a great supposition as John's.

What did they actually see and hear? Individual and mass or group healings beyond imagination, I suspect.

I am citing some verse examples from the Gospel of Mark. Notice Mark 1:32-34:

And at even, when the sun did set, they brought unto him all that were diseased, and them that were possessed with demons. And all the city was gathered together at the door. And he healed many that

*were sick of various diseases, and
cast out demons; and suffered not
the demons to speak, because they
knew him*

Look also at more mass healings and miracles in
Mark 3:10:

> *For he had healed many;
> insomuch that they pressed upon
> him for to touch him, as many as
> had plagues. And unclean spirits,
> when they saw him, fell down
> before him and cried [out]...*

Notice the words in both verses; he healed many,
and he had healed many...

Nothing I have cited thus far is an example of
an individual healing, and there are other mass
healing verses as well.

For the sake of impression, I point to a *man
delivered from a demon in a synagogue* in Mark
1:23-26, *a paralyzed man* let down through a roof
in Mark two, *the man in a synagogue, healed of a
withered arm* in Mark three, *the demon filled man
having legions cast out* near Gadera in Mark five, or
even *the synagogue ruler's daughter revived from*

death in Mark 5:22.

Another example of group or mass healings that cannot be numbered is noticed in Mark 6:54-56:

> *"And when they were come out of the ship, straightway they knew him, and ran through that whole region round about, and began to carry about in beds those that were sick, where they heard he was. And wheresoever he entered, into villages, or city, or country, they laid the sick in the street, and besought him that they might touch if it were but the border of his garment: and as many as touched him were made whole."*

Whew! In today's world, it would be like healing the entire sick ward in a hospital, and sending them all home well.

The Greek Testament terms in those verses of Mark 6:54-56, are *"too kraspe'doo himati'oo autoo,"* coming to us in Anglicized form as "the border of his garment."

The Septuagint translation uses the same

Greek term in Numbers 15:38-42 (kraspe'da), and it refers to the special garment commanded the Jewish male to be worn with "fringes" (TziTzit). The people were reaching to touch his prayer shawl fringes. We believe that Jesus' miracles, healings, and exorcisms were real, and not exaggerated.

The Hebrew Bible gives various details about Moses and the prophets working signs, wonders, and miracles under God's authority (see Exodus 4:28-31). It's also known that exorcism, or expelling demons, happened in the Hebrew Bible.

Notice, in 1Samuel 16:14-23, *wherein it is written that when David played the harp, the evil spirit was exorcised from Saul.*

But Judaism does stress, that its monotheistic God has absolute and sovereign control in all matters.

Power over demons was attributed to King Solomon in Exodus RABBAH. '*Many spirits and demons did Solomon vanquish,*' although the power deserted him later in life, because, as it is said,

'*Until Solomon sinned, he ruled over the demons.*'

Although belief in and about demons have played a relatively unimportant role in Judaism, rabbinic literature does not deny their existence.

יֵשׁוּעַ

and Parables

Chapter 12

Jesus and Parables

There is a pool of Hebrew sayings (parables), numbering near 5,000 and about 800 of them are known as king parables. Many sages drew from them and used them as a teaching tool.

Readers of the Christian Bible also know that Jesus used parables in his teachings quite liberally. *But what is a parable...* and how does such a tool enhance teaching? We should examine the Greek word parable and consider its meaning in the sayings of Jesus.

A concordance lists the word parable/s as being found in approximately 62 Bible verses of the K. J. Version. The coded Greek number is 3850, and comes from the words *para*, and *ballo* (2 Greek words), with listed meanings; *to throw alongside* [for comparison], *similitude, comparison. adage, figure, proverb.*

Parables were sometimes a short simple story which communicated a moral or spiritual truth.

Some parables used figurative or symbolic language to convey a particular lesson. Jesus was not the first to teach with parables.

We who are Christians somehow fail to recognize the abundance of parables in our Bible. For instance the book called Proverbs. In Hebrew it reads: *Mishlei Shlomoh ven David, melekh Yisrael. It could also have been translated, Parables of Solomon Son of David, King of Israel.* The term rendered "proverbs" could also have been translated "parables."

The particular word *mashal*, and its plural form *mishlei*, is noted in the Hebrew Concordance under number 4912. When we realize that the so called Book of Proverbs, is in truth, a book of parables, we can grasp a significant truth, namely that 31 chapters of Proverbs is really a book of Parables. And what shall we then say of Ecclesiastes and the Song of Songs?

This is not surprising however, since 1Kings 4:32 relates concerning Solomon; *he spake three thousand parables and his songs were a thousand and five.* This is why I said long before Jesus came along, parables were used by Hebrew thinkers and teachers as teaching tools.

Jesus was following in a great tradition of teaching. The Talmud expresses parables in many lessons, and we accept that many of them were part of an unwritten oral tradition.

Solomon's father, King David, was also quite a literary genius because of Divine inspiration. Sages say that he composed all the Psalms drawing upon the works of ten psalmists-including Moses, who wrote Psalm 90-100.

Rashi says that David incorporated them all into Psalms. One view in the Talmud conveyed that David was the author of them all, presumably drawing upon ideas and weaving them into his own compositions. Even the non Hebraic prophet Balaam, made use of parables in his prophecy found in Numbers 23:7, 24:3, and Numbers 24:20. He realized that he couldn't curse Israel. He envisioned the goodliness of Jacob's tents and tabernacles, and saw that Amalek would perish. God opened his eye, allowing the Presence to come upon him, even though Balaam was willing to try and assist Balak. The book of Numbers mentions his parables. *The wisdom of God as expressed by the sages is given in parables.*

My studies indicate a two fold purpose for parables, although some may contest my findings. Matthew chapter thirteen and verse three, wrote about the huge crowds which followed Jesus saying;

...great multitudes were gathered

*together unto him...and he spake
many things unto them in
parables.*

Jesus also was using the parable as a teaching tool for "multitudes." Within that chapter alone, there exists *seven parables*; a parable of the sower, parable of the wheat and tares, parable of the mustard seed, parable of the hidden leaven, parable of the hidden treasure, parable of the pearl of great price, and parable of the cast net and the sea. *He linked each parable to a movement of God in the earth which he called, "the kingdom of Heaven."*

According to the author of Matthew 13:35, that writer felt that Jesus use of parables was a fulfillment of a prophetic utterance made by Asaph (rewritten by King David), and located in Psalm 78:2,

> *I will utter things which have been
> kept secret from the foundation of
> the world. I will utter riddles from
> antiquity, which we have heard
> and know, and our fathers told us.*

That translation from Psalm 78 states that parables were passed down from fathers to sons, and revealed riddles from ancient history of the Jewish people. The various details given in Psalm 78 are indeed applicable to Israel's history.

According to Rabbi Hirsch-*the events of Israel's history are parables-object lessons for all times. The principles demonstrated by these events serve to explain the otherwise inexplicable riddles of subsequent Jewish history.*

Truly, Psalm 78 reveals both the success and the failure of some of Israel's people. One segment of Israel receives the reproof of Psalm 78:37,

> *For their heart was not right with Him, neither were they stedfast in His covenant.*

Another verse wrote in Psalm 78:17,

> *But they continued more to sin against Him, to rebel against the Most High in the desert.*

Such comments indicate that Israel's people and existence itself, is sort of a riddle of ancient times.

Why should there exist among a holy people, a population segment whose hearts were not right with God, or those who were not stedfast with Him and His covenant? The Fact is, within any religious tradition or group, there are folks who do not live up to the faith, as well as some who may not be faithful to the cause. But, in Israel's case, because of the many miracles and wonders which He manifest for that people, it seems more of a riddle than usual. These were the Holy people to whom the Lord gave the Divine "oracles" or the *logia* (logia-words) of God.

The same Psalms chapter in Psalm 78:10, wrote; *lo shamru berith Elohim, oov Torahto meianu lalechet.* "They did not guard the covenant of God, and His Torah they refused to follow."

The riddle deepens, but three things, we notice from the chapter: 1. A *people within a people,* 2. *Parables or riddles as a teaching tool,* 3. *Fathers passing down to children many sayings and traditions.*

Reading further in Matthew 13:14, Jesus adds another reference from a prophecy in Isaiah, combining it with Psalm 78:2. This addition adds more insight upon the twofold purpose of parable teaching...

> *By hearing ye shall hear, and shall not understand, and seeing ye shall see and not perceive* (Isaiah 6:9).

Thus, a segment of people within a people, the ones whose heart is not right with God, or do not keep His covenant, or rebel constantly against the Most High, do not have a fruitful understanding of things of God. This is because of the parable teaching tool. At the same time, those who have a heart right with God, and love Him with all the heart, mind, and soul, while keeping His teaching, will listen to the parable. It will then sink into the heart and they will grasp the message which God sends to them.

To one, the parable is an enigma, but to the other the parable becomes a blessing. Why else would Jesus say,

> *Because to you it is given to know the mysteries of the kingdom of heaven, but to them it is not given* (Matthew 13:11).

This makes the prophecy of Isaiah so enlightening. In them is fulfilled the prophecy, which says;

> *For this peoples heart is waxed gross, and their ears are dull of hearing, and their eyes they have closed, lest at any time they should see with their eyes, and hear with their ears, and should understand with their heart, and should repent, and I should heal them.*

In the wisdom of God, *the parable is designed to enlighten and assist the understanding of the sincere person who puts trust in God. Conversely, the parable is designed in the wisdom of God, to confuse the non-repentant religionist,* thus keeping him on the outer edge of faith, even though that one travels with a believing group. Until they repent, no parable will ever hold true significance for them.

A popular saying with Jesus was: *"He that hath ears to hear let him hear."* That phrase is located in Matthew 13, about 4 times. It's found elsewhere also, but is located in the first chapter of the Book of Revelation in the message to the seven churches of Asia. Those prophetic church admonitions are given a total of seven times by the Holy Spirit. Yet, the text plainly says that JESUS is doing the talking. *You see, to Jesus, hearing was not hearing unless the words were permitted to sink down into the ears or heart* (Luke 9:44).

Parables should be meditated upon, applying the moral and spiritual truths to ones own life. But, parables are not necessarily designed to teach theology, rather they teach us principles of the kingdom of heaven in this world.

A normal first response regarding my comment about parables having a secondary purpose is; it seems so unfair that the wisdom of God would conceal a parable meaning from one group or segment of a group, and yet bring enlightenment to another segment of the same group.-Remember though, Jesus had spoken of eyes which did not see, and in that same conversation (Matthew 13), spoke of eyes which did see and ears which did hear. Blessings were upon those who saw and who heard.

Perhaps, the 11th principle of Judaism as expressed by Maimonides, and also found in the liturgy of the morning prayers, would bring better understanding of why God withholds from one while blessing another. *He rewards man with kindness according to his deeds. He sends evil to the wicked according to his wickedness.*

The equation only seems unfair, until we learn that God deals with rebellious humankind in the same measure as mankind approaches God. The measure for measure outlay can be changed by humility and repentance. A scripture verse which supports the measure for measure outlay is located in Psalm 18:26-27, saying; *"With the pure You act purely, and with the perverse You are wily, It is You who deliver lowly folk, but haughty eyes You humble"* (JPS Hebrew-English Tanach).

Jesus' comments in Matthew 13:16, clarify that God will heal and restore those who do repentance. Their eyes, ears, and hearts will become fruitful in understanding. This is true, not only about parables, but about any teachings of the Kingdom of Heaven: understanding eventually comes to the "pure in heart." Jesus had told his immediate disciples;

> *But blessed are your eyes for they see: and your ears for they hear. For verily I say unto you, that many prophets and righteous men have desired to see those things which ye see, and have not seen them, and to hear those things which ye hear, and have not heard them.*

Being called and invited into the "inner circle" has a way of separating folks from other folks.

Jesus' parable about the kingdom of heaven being like a treasure hidden in a field (Matthew 13:44), which when a man finds, he sells all he has to be able to acquire the money to purchase the property, and then with great joy purchases the property and its treasure, reveals an amazing concept.

In those times the property owner had legal rights to the treasure also. Some things are worth owning for yourself, no matter what the cost. *The treasured things of God's kingdom are available, but who is willing to pay the price to have the field and its treasure?* Only the humble and pure of heart, would think that the kingdom of heaven had such tremendous value. No-one but a seeker of God, could imagine the value of a field with "hidden treasure."

We must not forget the principle of measure for measure, and we shouldn't fail to realize that there are scriptural limitations to some things. Notice a wonderful passage in Psalm 103:10

> *He has not dealt with us according to our sins, nor has He repaid us according to our iniquities, for as high as the heavens are above the earth, so has His kindness prevailed over those who revere Him.*

The compassionate Father, who loves His people, never gives them a full measure of reward for transgressions, when they repent, lest justice should overrule mercy, and destroy the holy people.

> *Aren't we glad that His full anger is not aroused, and time is granted for repentance?* As it is written:

> *The mercy of the Lord is from everlasting to everlasting upon them that fear Him and His righteousness unto children's children* (Psalm 103:17).

It's certain why the prophecy was given for Israel, in spite of its sins and transgressions; *"I am the Lord, I change not; therefore ye sons of Jacob are not consumed."*

Because God didn't fully recompense His children, Israel exists yet today. And not only Israel, but all who haven't fully obeyed God in every detail.

All who cling to Him, will not experience the full measure of His wrath.
Amen!

ANCIENT HEBREW WISDOM

"NONE

IS POOR

SAVE HIM

THAT LACKS

KNOWLEDGE"

Did

ישוע

Use Hebrew

Or Aramaic

In the Greek Gospels

Chapter 13

Did Jesus Use Hebrew or Aramaic in the Greek Gospels

Language barriers have always caused problems in communications between humans. This is especially true in regard to religious documents which have to be translated from source language into receptor languages.

Arguments have been made by scholars as to the actual language Jesus used to convey his teachings. Since the scripture says "He came unto his own and his own received him not " (John 1:11), we confidently affirm that the Jewish people of Jesus' own land [Israel], were well versed in Hebrew language according to John 19:20, or at least in three languages, to be able to read the inscription on the cross in Hebrew, Greek, and Latin.

Some scholars have asserted that Hebrew means Aramaic in the New Testament. The source document evidence does not support such contention. Jesus may have made use of Aramaic or even Greek from time to time, as well as Hebrew.

But the Aramaic theory is unwarranted in light of all the internal evidence suggesting otherwise. Semitic word mix in "Shemitic" languages is normal since the loan word value of words incorporated into Hebrew exceeds ten per cent. It's noted in loan words like mammon [money], and used yet today from Chaldean into Hebrew. *People assume too much at times, and New Testament word mix has caused many a good scholar to err.* This is seem easily by comparing the actual number of Aramaic verses in the Old Testament, which is about 250 verses, to the actual number of Hebrew verses, which is near 23,000.

Certain things stood out to me as I read the Gospels and the Book of Acts. Verses like Luke 23:38. John 19:20, and Acts 26:14, all mention the use of the Hebrew language or tongue. The narrative about the inscription on the cross [tree], and the language used from heaven to earth, while Jesus conversed with Saul of Tarsus, on the Damascus Road, was convincing. **I had heard that Hebrew meant Aramaic, but why did manuscript copies say that Jesus spoke in Hebrew? If Aramaic was intended to be the translation rendering, what happened?**

My personal investigation of the Greek manuscript copies showed that the Greek text did not give a Greek spelling equating the word Aramaic. **Why didn't scholars believe what was written in the manuscripts?** *Surely, this was not a form of intellectual dishonesty. Regardless of the reasons why it was asserted that Hebrew meant Aramaic, I knew better, after looking long and hard at actual manuscript copies. Such discoveries caused me to delve deeper into the study of Hebrew and compare with Greek readings. I concluded that the King James scholars were correct in rendering the term "Hebrew" in those verses.*

But, on the other hand *I began to find out all kinds of interesting things relative to long established English "traditions," and erring links of a nature not consistent with accurate translation.* Examples are words like Lucifer, Calvary, Devils [instead of demons], Easter, James [instead of Jacob), and even the word Jesus. This caused me a gentle jolt when learning that those words were just not consistent with the Hebrew and Greek texts from whence they were claimed to have originated. It was stunning and disappointing when I realized that transliteration and translation terms weren't so precise. Five of those terms didn't even belong in an English readers Bible, and one is a poor rendering of a Hebrew into Greek to English transliteration. *But, the tradition still stands in spite of the facts.*

Hebrew words and names abound throughout the New testament. The Hebrew-Aramaic word mix is evident in the Gospels, and diligent Hebrew students know as previously stated that the long time Aramaic word mix consists of over 10% incorporated into Hebrew. Shemitic languages are known to have three basic commonalities. 1. Some shared word meanings, 2. Guttural sounds, 3. Mostly three root consonants. This may have been what threw some scholars and teachers off track, since the Gospel of Mark contains some Aramaic terms.

However, Mark and the other three gospels also contain purely Hebrew words. Examples are noted by Matthew 28:20, Mark 16:20, Luke 24:53, and John 21:25. Each of the Four Gospels ends with the English translation; AMEN. I also recall that a prayer endorsed by Jesus in Matthew 6:13, ends with an AMEN. Wow! King James Version translators saved 5 AMENS for us from the Greek Gospel text copies, by transliterating them from Greek into the English "amen," rather than translating them into an English word. So, what is the Hebraic word "amen" doing hiding in a Greek text?

This is an evidence of a Hebrew conversation taking place within a Greek narrative. Further investigation reveals that within the four gospels alone, over 100 "amens" appear. But, it's obscured by the fact that English translators rendered them verily or truly. ***So, why are Hebrew amens occurring in the mouth of Jesus, in a Greek document, as he talks to his 12 and 70 disciples?*** Fact is, that "amen" is an ancient Hebrew word, and the New Testament, contains plenty of Hebrew words and thoughts. The story and information about Jesus in our Gospels was evidently turned into Greek for the sake of evangelization.

Some grammarians have put periods in the wrong place in regard to the Hebrew "amen." Sentences do not start with amen among Hebrew speakers. Amen is like the word selah: pause, meditate, think about it. Always look at what was said in the Bible text before the amen occurs.

The Spirit of the Lord teaches us in our renewed nature, that amen is a response. Have you ever been in a church service when something good was said by a speaker, and a congregant sounds out, Amen? A Hebrew-Greek scholar acquaintance of mine once said; *[gospel] evangelists have tended to treat amen as a Greek word.*

In the Hebrew Bible (O.T.), the amen response appears, and in some cases, a double amen, just as it occurs in the Gospel of John. It's there that we find the translation phrases, verily, verily. But our "amen" ends a particular matter. It's the same at the closing of every prayer. Amen, amen, and so be it.

Recent scholarship and more profound studies, discovery of the Bar Kochba letters, the Hebrew Ben Sira (Ecclesiasticus) of the Dead Sea scrolls, and language of the Jewish sages, show that it is accepted that most people were fluent in Hebrew. One professor noted for his studies at the Hebrew University, wrote over twenty years ago: that the Pentatuech [five Torah Books], was translated into Aramaic for the benefit of the lower strata of the population. The parables of the Rabbinic literature, on the other hand, were delivered in Hebrew in all periods. There is thus no ground for assuming that Jesus did not speak in Hebrew; and when we are told [Acts 21:40], that Paul spoke Hebrew, we should take this piece of information at face value.

It was also said; ***The question of the spoken language is especially important for understanding the doctrines of Jesus.*** *There are sayings of Jesus which can be rendered both into Hebrew and Aramaic; but there are some which can only be rendered into Hebrew, and none of them can be rendered only in Aramaic.* **One can thus demonstrate the Hebrew origins of the Gospels by retranslating them into Hebrew.**

Studies of Rabbinic literature reveal that that

there existed a "pool" of about 5,000 parables, and 800 of them are known as king parables. Only a scant number of them are known in Aramaic, but virtually all of them are written in Hebrew. Jesus, David, and Solomon all used parables to teach. Jesus and many sages drew from this "pool" of parables to teach.

It has been reported by some *that Martin Luther once said in reference to the Hebrew language or customs,* **that the Hebrews drink from the main pool, the Greeks from the stream that flows from it, and the Latins from a pool downstream.** Another scholar has said, Hebrew enables us to see the Old Testament from inside instead of peering through the telescope of a version.

Those comments help the Bible reader to *appreciate the value and importance of knowledge of Hebrew language and culture.* Assuming that Luther's insight is correct, we are only left to wonder, **which pool are we drinking from today, since we are so far removed from Hebrew language, custom, and culture, as well as the passing of so much time in history?**

Traditional views of the rabbis expressed that Hebrew is the language of prayer and recital of the shema (Deuteronomy 6:4), and the term

lashon hakodesh

לְשׁוֹן הַקוֹדֶשׁ

Hebrew ~ The Holy Tongue

describes it as *"the holy tongue."* The rabbis also relate that one may pray in ANY language since God knows them all, and the lack of knowledge of Hebrew, should not prevent a Jew [or anyone] from praying in his native tongue.

The Gospel of Matthew contains a famous prayer given by Jesus, to answer a request: Lord, teach us to pray as John also taught his disciples (Luke 11:1). The formula given is complete in Matthew 6:9-13, and has the tradition of being called *The Lord's Prayer*. That title may have come about because the prayer is directed to the Lord in heaven; maybe it should be called the disciples prayer. The student had asked, teach us to pray... not teach us HOW to pray. Evidently the Baptizer was instructing his followers in some prayer behavior.

In the disciples prayer, the Greek text uses the terms *pater umon* (pater humon), which comes into English as "Father of us," or "Our Father." By using the suggested pattern of turning Greek words back into Hebrew, we capture one Hebrew phrase, which is known as

Avinu

אָבִינוּ

That phrase is famous and well known among Jews today and for generations back. The Hebrew or Jewish mindset immediately associates Avinu with the same word appearing in much Hebrew liturgy and Jewish prayers. Many traditional prayers use the phrase *Avinu malkenu* (our Father our king). It occurs over and over on *Yom Kippur* (Day of Atonement), and begins the prayers which rise repeatedly from worshipper's lips, as *they petition God to listen, and open the gates of heaven.*

Talmudic sources assign some of the lines of the Avinu malkenu to *Rabbi Akiva* about 40-135 A.D., who made the prayer for rain in a time of drought. Over a period of time the formula was repeated with other requests, until today, some 44 supplications are linked to Avinu malkenu, and used by some congregations.

The word Avinu was used by both Akiva and Jesus. We know that the Avinu pattern affected

Jews for many generations, and we also know that Jesus used the Avinu (Our Father) prayer for an example in what we call the Lord's Prayer.

Even today prayers on Yom Kippur, contain many requests in the Avinu to be inscribed in the Book of Life, with requests for His blessing.

I will give a Hebrew example of the prayer here, and my translation follows-

אָבִינוּ שֶׁבַּשָּׁמַיִם יִתְקַדַּשׁ שְׁמֶךָ

תָּבֹא מַלְכוּתֶךָ יֵעָשֶׂה רְצוֹנְךָ כְּמוֹ

בַשָּׁמַיִם כֵּן בָּאָרֶץ

אֶת־לֶחֶם חֻקֵּנוּ תֶּן־לָנוּ הַיּוֹם

וּסְלַח־לָנוּ אֶת־חֹבוֹתֵנוּ כַּאֲשֶׁר סָלַחְנוּ

גַּם־אֲנַחְנוּ

לְחַיָּבֵינוּ: וְעַל־תְּבִיאֵנוּ לִידֵי נִסָּיוֹן כִּי

אִם־חַלְּצֵנוּ

מִן־הָרָע כִּי לְךָ הַמַּמְלָכָה וְהַגְּבוּרָה

וְהַתִּפְאֶרֶת

לְעוֹלְמֵי עוֹלָמִים אָמֵן

MY TRANSLATION INTO ENGLISH

Commonly Referred To As "The Lord's Prayer"

Our Father which is in the heavens, holy is Your name.

Your kingdom come Your will be done, like in the heavens, so in the earth.

Give us today our daily food, and forgive us our debts, when we also forgive our debtors,

And don't lead us into the hands of temptation, except You rescue us from the evil.

For Yours is the kingdom, and the might, and the glory, for ever and ever. Amen.

In this prayer the Matthew 6:9 phrase, "hallowed be thy name," refers to the *sanctity of God*, as expressed in the Divine names. The similar terminology, sanctification of the Name, or *kiddush haShem*, as known in Hebrew, refers to an action wherein an individual is willing to be martyred for the sake of heaven, thus honoring God. It's not suicide, which is forbidden in Judaism. Rather, it connects to the command which says in Deuteronomy 6:6, *"love the Lord ...your God...with all your soul."*

One must be willing to love Him, even if He would take thy soul. This was expressed in the Book of Job, who said during his trials; *"though He slay me, yet will I trust in Him"* (Job 13:15).

The Lord's Prayer also emphasizes a request for God's kingdom to come. This is an aspect of God's rule in the hearts of men of this world. When a person studies and examines Jewish liturgy such as a "prayer book," it's not hard to find constant clues that relate to many things which Jesus taught or how he instructed his students to pray.

The more one knows about the Jewishness of Jesus, the more capable that person becomes in understanding the Greek New Testament and the many Hebraic teachings of Jesus.

Add to that knowledge, that there is absolutely no early church tradition for a primitive Aramaic gospel. *We find no solid reasons to assume that Jesus didn't deliver his parables in Hebrew, when speaking to the masses.*

Neither do we accept the "replacement" theory, which suggests that the term Aramaic actually means Hebrew, nor that Hebrew means Aramaic.

A person familiar with the Greek manuscript spelling of the terms knows that the Greek letters which represent Aramaic, are just not there within the texts of the verses claimed to support the theory that "Hebrew means Aramaic."

The TANAKH... is the Hebrew Bible,
the Quintessential Sacred Text.
The first five Books of this comprise the Torah
(or Pentateuch) the Core Sacred Writings of
the Ancient Jews, Traditionally written
by Moses under Divine Inspiration

Knowing

ישוע

and

His Bible

Chapter 14

Knowing Jesus ~ and His Bible

I recently heard an excellent Sunday morning message from the pastor of a large church, in which he stated a couple of books had been written by individuals who recognized that their information about Jesus was largely inaccurate, so they began to study the gospel stories. In time, after investigating the Gospels, new and correct conclusions were formed about Jesus. *This is often the case.*

Fact is that much information about the Lord is based on traditions, opinions, and interpretive conclusions not based on internal sources [gospels], or proper historical references.

Some Christians lack knowledge because they have not fully read the entire Bible, or they have not been sufficiently exposed to balanced teaching and preaching by well schooled leaders. At times it may have been because they chose to be part of an assembly with a wave of excitement, music, or other interesting features of Christianity. But knowing the real Jesus is more important, than knowing all the interesting features.

There is a better way to know about Jesus, better than experience, better than knowing what others say about him. The best way to know about Jesus is to scrutinize HIS OWN WORDS. After many years of preaching to my flock (congregation), I realized that many of them didn't seem to know what Jesus believed or said. They seemed to know what Paul said, and what Peter said, and about the letters to the Churches, but only a few seemed to really know exactly what Jesus said. God enabled me to devise a plan to remedy the problem, and based it on Paul's words in 1Timothy 4:13- *"Till I come, give attendance to reading..."*

I decided to publicly read all the words of Jesus in the entire New Testament, and used a red letter edition of the King James Version as a guide to get us all on the same page. I used our ministry staff to do the readings in public services, although it took numerous services. The ministers and I completed the task, and the people were well informed from the pulpit, as to what Jesus had taught and spoken. What a great way to get to know Jesus-by learning HIS WORDS. *Some folks focus on spiritual experiences and they may feel it more needful to have what they call a godly relationship, but if Jesus is God's last day spokesman as indicated in Hebrews 1:2, then should we not know*

exactly what he taught and said to his followers? Part of knowing him, is knowing what he taught and said-what he expects of us. *Knowing which Bible Jesus used or read, indicates how as a human, his character developed, and what he believed.*

Have you ever stopped to consider; what Bible Jesus read? Given the sense of urgency placed upon Bible reading by many fundamental Christians, and the emphasis placed on particular English language versions, it might help to know which Bible Jesus would have read. Of course you realize by now, that I've presented a loaded question, which is designed to make one think. The truth is, no matter what you or I think, the man Jesus has never read any Christian Bible Version.

We must recognize that all he learned or knew from boyhood to manhood was learned from study and meditation upon the words of his Heavenly Father, combined with the instruction of parents and teachers, and interaction with other knowledgeable Jews.

It is common knowledge in the Jewish community about the memorization capacity of sages and scholars. Some of them had memorized every verse in the 5 Torah books, and could have written by memory alone, an entire *Pentateuch Scroll*. But that was forbidden, since each scribe was to have a Torah copy before him to look at for precision, when making a new Torah scroll. *Nothing was left to chance, and every copy must be made according to very rigid rules, which assured accuracy and sanctification regarding the Divine Name.*

I recall reading about the *Vilna Gaon*, (Elijah Ben Solomon), who as a child prodigy had memorized every letter and word in the Talmud. When one realizes the vast and broad scope of Talmudic material, it's remarkable indeed that a thirteen year old was able to commit it all to memory. Especially when one considers that the 5 books of Torah, with all its words contain 304, 805 letters. Comparing that detail about the Talmud and the 63 tractates therein, we can appreciate the work and effort required to memorize both the Tanakh and the Talmud.

The explanations of the Oral Torah had been memorized over all of 1,500 years, before it was finally permitted to be written down. And, much biblical information was also committed to memory by Godly parents, who passed it down to children. Surely, Jesus had learned many things through his own studious efforts, as well as what was passed down by sages and family. Today, it is known that the *Babylonian Talmud* contains 20 volumes.

Even during times of extreme testing and confrontation, he often cited the phrase, "it is written." Those references were to verses written by Moses. Before and during the times of Jesus, generations of students, had memorized, studied, and passed down volumes of information from the Torah (law), the prophets, and the writings. How could he have possibly known what was written if he never had read it?

Jewish tradition has a very interesting way of making reference to the *Hebrew Bible*. By defining the **3 sections (divisions), of the Hebrew scrolls**, and giving them their Hebrew names, a new name is gained which represents the Jewish body of sacred scripture which we call "Bible." The first word is **TORAH**, which specifies *the first five books of Moses. Torah is generally rendered law, teaching, or instruction.* That word begins with the letter T. So, we set aside the " T," to help form the new word, and soon add the next letter from another section of Jesus' Bible.

The second section of the *Jewish Bible* is called **NAVIIM**, *and means prophets.* So lets add that letter to the letter " T." Now with TN, we have 2 Hebrew consonant letters which represent 2 sections of the Jewish writings, Torah and Naviim (law and prophets). In a moment by taking the first three letters of the Hebrew names for 3 sections of scripture, we will have a new name for the Jewish scripture which Jews everywhere understand.

The third section is called **KETUVIM**, *which means "writings."* **The three sections of the Jewish Bible then, are law, prophets, and writings**. Now, let's put each first letter of each Hebrew word on the same line and form the representative term for the Jewish Bible; TNK.

When our Jewish friends refer to the Hebrew Bible, or what Christians claim is the Old Testament, they use the 3 letters which represent the Hebrew names of the 3 sections of their Bible; TNK. It is vocalized by means of various spellings: *Tenach, Tanakh, Tanach.*

Jesus referred to the Tanakh in Luke 24:44, which wrote in part: *"that all things might be fulfilled, which were written in the law of Moses, and the prophets, and in the Psalms concerning me."* The Psalms are part of the section considered "writings."

At this point in our lesson, it is necessary to inform Christian readers that *among Jewish educators, the section called the TORAH, has been considered given a higher position of honor and greater inspiration then the other 2 sections of the inspired Hebrew scriptures.*

Where is authority for this? It's based on verses in Deuteronomy 34:10-11, with Divine revelation and confirmation granted him by the Lord:

> *And there never arose a prophet again in Israel like Moses, whom the Lord knew face to face, for all the signs and wonders, which the Lord sent him to do in the land of Egypt, to Pharaoh and his servants, and to all his land.*

Those verses, when compared to Numbers 12:6-8, show that Moses was not inferior in any way to any prophet, seer, visionary, or dreamer. Whether awake or asleep, Moses could speak to God face to face (*panim el panim*), or mouth to mouth (*peh el peh*). He didn't need a dream or vision or trance. I suggest it was possible, because of his extreme humility as noted in Numbers 12:3. It has a nagging oddity about it, that one section has a higher degree of inspiration, but after all, if Moses was the greatest of all prophets ever to rise in Israel, it makes sense that since Torah wrote this about Moses. Those teachings come from a man who did not see or prophesy in part, and are complete.

I have wondered at times why Christians don't attach more honor to the words of Jesus in theology. **The 4 Gospels contain all that he said and done, and he personally stated: "heaven and earth shall pass away, but my words shall not pass away" (Matthew 24:35). Yet, it seems on many matters, that the letters and epistles to churches are held in higher esteem then the words of the one whom Christians have called "Lord."**

Perhaps, *many theological hangups would have been avoided, if the words of Jesus had been given priority. After all, why call we him Lord, Lord, and do not the things which **he** said?*

Jesus emphasized the Law of Moses, and always upheld it. That is why he could say *"heaven and earth shall pass away, but my words shall not pass away."* He knew that scripture could not be broken. He knew that God's word was forever established in the heavens.

As far as I know, Jesus never tried to change or refute anything that Moses taught. However, in certain circumstances he openly disagreed with some Pharisaic INTERPRETATIONS of the words of Moses.

We can be assured that Jesus knew the entire Tanakh (from Genesis to Malachi). The gospel narratives show him often quoting or referencing verses from those sources. *But, we also recognize after much study and comparisons, that...*

> *Jesus seemed to be quite familiar with all the oral explanations of the Hebrew traditions, and evidently was able to discuss it intelligently with experts at the Temple, when he was only 12 years old.*
> (See Luke 2:42-52).

ישוע

and Money

Chapter 15

Jesus and Money

In Matthew 6:29, Jesus made reference to Solomon:

And yet I say unto you, that even Solomon in all his glory, was not arrayed like one of these...

In a previous verse he had commented; "consider the lilies of the field, they toil not, neither do they spin". The reason he had mentioned Solomon's wealth and glory, was his concern about treasure, wealth, or money, becoming the driving force behind everyday life and existence, among the people of God..

In Matthew 6:19-34 (15 verses), Jesus emphasized that God would provide for every necessity, of his children. He focused on teachings his students, to NOT allow mammon to become the master of life. He said;

"You cannot serve God and

mammon" (Matthew 6:24).

The term "mammon," is a Chaldean loan word incorporated into Hebrew, and is yet in use today. It means "money." In pursuit of the regular necessities for life (food, drink, shelter, clothing), Jesus had warned, no man can serve two masters. Keep every priority in order, is a true spiritual mantra.

He alluded to Solomon and all his glory with his kingly raiment. At the same time, without negating sensible preparation and planning, he asserted; "consider the lilies." His comparative analysis of flowers of the fields with Solomon's raiment, and glory, showed a concern of God even for nature itself. His words; "take therefore no thought for the morrow," made in regard to eating, drinking or clothing; is reference to anxiousness, and not to sensible preparation. Jesus taught people to trust God and not to worry. If God clothed the grass of the fields in natural beauty, why would He not clothe the children of faith, who are far more important than fading flowers?

That formula is not inconsistent with the Tanakh (Hebrew Bible). It was written in Proverbs 23:4,

> *Labor not to be rich; cease from thine own wisdom.*

One's total energies should be well concentrated to serve God first, and things can fall into place. But, as in everything else, we must have balance in our ambitions. Maybe that's why the Tanakh also wrote in Ecclesiastes 10:19:

> *A feast is made for laughter, and wine maketh merry, but MONEY answereth all [things]*.

When people have money, it can be used to have a feast, throw a party, and thereby produce temporary joy and happiness. Proper use of money, does provide answers to some problems.

Folks often have said that money is the root of all evil. That's a falsehood! The Christian Bible wrote,

> *The love of money is the root of all evil* (1 Timothy 6:10).

To covet money is a form of idolatry. So, loving God with all the heart, soul, and strength, is the balance and understanding for how to apply the use and desire for money.

The author of the Epistle of Yakov (epistle of Jakob/James), in his letter to the twelve tribes scattered abroad, wrote:

> *Go to now you rich men, weep and howl for your miseries that shall come upon you...* (James 1:1 and James 5:1).

He stressed that the long time wealth of the wicked (gold and silver), was accumulated by evil practices; fraud, dishonesty, and slaughter (Yakov 5:1-6). He reminds Christians who have been similarly oppressed by evil and rich masters, to be patient, and recall that the prophets had austerity and suffering heaped upon them, and to follow their example of enduring patiently.

The example used in reference to Solomon and his glory, is not the only time Jesus alluded to him. In Matthew 12:42, Jesus shares his knowledge about Solomon, and the Queen of Sheba. She came from the utmost part of the earth to investigate the rumored wisdom of Solomon. Thus, Jesus pointed to the glory of Solomon and the wisdom of Solomon.

The biblical account of Solomon and the Queen of Sheba is given in 1Kings 10:1-14. The Tanakh wrote, that in the same year when the Queen of Sheba visited Solomon, his wealth was increased by 666 talents of gold, among other valued items. The Queen of Sheba gifted Solomon with 120 talents of gold herself.

There are conflicting opinions about the

weight or weight value of 1 talent of gold or silver in the time of Solomon. The term talentum is found in Latin, and in Greek, the talanton (talantov) is also found in that tongue as well.

In reference to the unit of weight used in Solomon's day to measure amounts of silver or gold, we find the Hebrew Bible term was (כִּכָּר) kikar, which K.J. Version scholars rendered "talent."

kikar (talent)

The Egyptian talent was approximately 60 pounds, a Babylonian talent was about 67 pounds, and a Greek talent was about 57 pounds. Some say that the New Testament talent was equal to 130 pounds.

I prefer to refer to the Hebrew- English translators foot notes on 1Kings 9:28, which states that a talent was approximately 64 pounds. Translators of the Orthodox Jewish scriptures seem quite knowledgeable about such details, and I am inclined to trust their opinions in many things, when Hebrew tradition and cuture are involved.

The word kikar in Hebrew, can be located in a

numbered concordance (#3603, and can mean, something round like a coin, or a loaf (bread). In today's world, we could imagine a gold or silver American Eagle, which in our custom, would have a weight value of one ounce. 1Kings 10:14 and 2Chronicles 9:13, both mention that Solomon received 666 talents of gold in one year.

Now, 666 talents of gold, was Solomon's income for one year. Weighing at 64 pounds per talent, equates 42, 624 pounds of gold. If we divide that number by 16 ounces per pound, we come up with 2,664 ounces of gold. In today's market value, we guestimate $1,700.00 per ounce: that represents four million, five hundred twenty eight thousand, eight hundred dollars ($4, 528, 800.00). Not bad at all for only one year of Solomon's personal wealth, counting only the 666 talents of gold. He had much more than that, and the conjectured number of ounces today would probably be based on the troy ounce weight of 12 ounces rather than 16 ounces.

The wisdom of Solomon given by God, brought revenue beyond belief to the king. We can only imagine the value and purchasing power of such gold three thousand years ago. ...Mind boggling indeed.

The Queen of Sheba came to Israel to investigate the rumored wisdom of Solomon. She was more than pleased when discovering the reports were true. The great woman was happy to hear, see, and learn from Solomon. So happy, that she gave him 120 talents of gold, and other valuable items. Her journey from the uttermost parts of the earth to hear the wisdom of Solomon was mentioned in Matthew 12:42, where Jesus contrasted it to a lack of Israeli interest by his generation, in his ministry and message of the kingdom of God.

His comments and comparisons were strikingly bold: "behold, a greater than Solomon is here." He had also said; "the Queen of the South shall rise up in the judgment with this generation; and shall condemn it." Was it proper for Jesus to view himself greater than Solomon? Was Jesus an egotist as a rabbi friend once told me? Was it appropriate to say, that this generation would be condemned in the judgment? Or was he on a Divine mission, knowing who he was, and who had sent him to the Israelis?

Jesus also dealt somewhat with the subject of "riches" in his parable or proverb about the "rich man" in Luke 12:16, saying:

> *The ground of a certain rich man,*
> *brought forth plentifully: And he*
> *thought within himself, saying,*
> *What shall I do, because I have no*

room where to bestow my fruits? And he said, this will I do: I will pull down my barns; and build greater; and there will I bestow all my fruits and all my goods. And I will say unto my soul, Soul, thou hast much goods laid up for many years; take thine ease, eat, drink, and be merry. But God said unto him, fool, this night thy soul shall be required of thee: then whose shall those things be, which thou hast provided?

Jesus assesses his own parable with certain and clear comprehension, saying;

> *So is he that layeth up treasure for himself, and is not rich toward God* (Luke 12:21).

Riches cannot detract from those who are "rich" toward God. Thus, ignoring soul preparation while in pursuit of wealth is unwise.

In other gospel verses Jesus advises followers to,

> *Sell that you have and give alms;*

provide for yourselves bags which wax not old, a treasure in the heavens that faileth not, where no thief approacheth, neither moth corrupteth. For where your treasure is, there will your heart be also.

Because Jesus knew that some people would allow money or riches to master them, he warned sternly against riches; saying in Mark 10:23: "How hardly shall they that have riches enter into the kingdom of God!" A similar warning is given in Mark 10:24:

Children, how hard it is for them that trust in riches to enter into the kingdom of God.

In other passages Jesus refers to the deceitfulness of riches which choke the word of God in ones life (Matthew 13:22).

Then in Luke 16:11, he says;

If therefore ye have not been faithful in the unrighteous mammon, who will commit to your trust the true riches?

Those words imply that people, who handle money properly in worldly matters, can also be trusted with accounting for spiritual matters. I firmly believe that God desires his children to be blessed and happy. He wants every necessity of life to be provided for them. And, the biblical concept of working for pay when possible, is truly applicable so that one may enjoy the fruits of his own labor, and is indeed a certain biblical principle.

The examples shown indicate that the Lord's blessing for His children is rich and generous. However, in times of wealth and prosperity, there is a tendency to warp the scriptures by using improper application and misrepresentation of Bible verses to prove a prosperity gospel promotion in order to entice people to contribute to causes.

On various instances, I have heard prosperity preachers, quote a verse from Deuteronomy 8:18, saying similar to the following: It is the Lord Your God which giveth you power to get wealth. Usually the purpose behind the quotation is to encourage people to have confidence in God, and to remind them that He will provide for prosperity. There is nothing wrong with building the level of trust of the people, in God's ability to provide in all situations.

Being a preacher and teacher of the biblical text myself, I often cringe when I hear someone misapply, or promote a translation of the Bible which is not exact, or leaves a lot to be desired, and offers no explanation of important detail.

In regard to Deuteronomy 8:18, I feel the need to point out a few matters, which I think are quite important to properly understand the verse.

1. The original text and context of the verse, speaks very specifically to Israel, and the whole assembly of that people by Moses, their leader.

2. Secondly, **a better translation could be made** which would not include the phrase *'power to get wealth,'* rather would say; *'strength to make wealth'*.

3. By omitting the rest of the verse when explaining its meaning, the whole purpose of "making wealth" is lost. The text says: *'that He may establish His covenant which He sware unto thy fathers, as it is this day'* (K.J. V.)

4. Lastly, the giver of the strength to make wealth is clearly identified as the Lord, the God of Israel numerous times in this 8th chapter. *The strength to make*

wealth is largely dependent upon obedience to His commands and words.

On the following page you will see my writing of *the actual Hebrew text*, and I *will then give my translation.*

My translation is in agreement with the wording of a English-Hebrew Bible in the translation terms, strength to make wealth, and establish His covenant.

When one reads the entire text and context, it makes better sense to translate as I have done on the following page.

Deuteronomy 8:18 *(In Original Hebrew)*

וְזָכַרְתָּ֙ אֶת־יְהוָ֣ה אֱלֹהֶ֔יךָ כִּ֣י ה֗וּא
הַנֹּתֵ֥ן לְךָ֛ כֹּ֖חַ לַעֲשׂ֣וֹת חָ֑יִל לְמַ֨עַן
הָקִ֤ים אֶת־בְּרִיתוֹ֙ אֲשֶׁר־נִשְׁבַּ֣ע
לַאֲבֹתֶ֔יךָ כַּיּ֥וֹם הַזֶּֽה

(My English Translation)

'So, you remember Yehovah your God: for it is He that gives you strength to make wealth, that He may establish His covenant which He swore for your fathers, as it is this day.'

Moses had warned the people in the previous verses that their hearts not become haughty because of the prosperity and favor which the Lord had provided Israel.

He told Israel in Deuteronomy 8:7 that God brought them to

> *...A good land, a land of brooks of water, of fountains and depths that*

spring out of valleys and hills: a land of wheat and barley, and vines and fig trees, and pomegranates; a land of oil, olive and honey. ...A land where thou shalt eat bread without scarceness. Thou shalt not lack anything in it; a land whose stones are iron, and out of whose hills thou mayest dig brass [copper].

Moses also said in God's name:

When thou hast eaten and art full, then thou shalt bless the Lord thy God for the good land which He hath given thee. Beware that thou forget not the Lord thy God, in not keeping His commandments- Lest when thou hast eaten and are full, and hast built goodly houses and dwelt therein; and when thy herds and flocks multiply, and thy silver and thy gold is multiplied, and all that thou hast is multiplied; Then thine heart be lifted up and thou forget the Lord thy God, which brought thee forth out of the land of Egypt, from the house of bondage; Who led thee through that great and terrible wilderness, wherein were fiery serpents, and scorpions, and drought, where there was no water: who brought thee forth water out of the rock of flint; Who fed thee in the wilderness with manna, which thy fathers knew not, that He might humble thee, and that He might prove thee, to do thee good at thy latter end; And thou say in thine heart, My strength and the might of my hand made me all this wealth. But thou shalt remember the Lord thy God, For it is He that giveth thee strength to make wealth, that He may establish His covenant which He swore to your fathers, as it is this day.

Now, after the reading of all these verses, we get the proper context, purpose, and textual meaning of the entire statement. All the things mentioned in the reading, define what "wealth" really was to the Israelites. Notice also *that both gold and silver were to be part of the wealth accumulation of the Israelites.*

The ability and strength to "make wealth," have agricultural blessings, and growth of flocks and herds, with multiplication of resources, was indeed the gift of the Lord, and *had a direct bearing on obedience to and observation of God's commands in the land of Israel.*

Deuteronomy 8:19-20, sums up the entire chapter, saying;

> *And it shall be, if thou do at all forget the Lord thy God, and walk after other gods, and serve them, and worship them, I testify against you this day that ye shall surely perish. 20 As the nations which the Lord destroyed before your face, so shall ye perish; because ye would not be obedient unto the voice of the Lord your God.*

We Christians have a tendency to take many verses out of context and redefine them or interpret them based upon our concepts of grace and favor shown us through the redemptive action of Yeshua God's anointed and chosen son. But, we should remember that the promise of prosperity given to Israel at the first, was not related to a gospel dispensation, rather to obedience to the teachings of the Lord as given by the hand of Moses.

It always seems convenient to take verses which we choose and desire to use to promote

Christian theology, and apply them to our situation. Yet, other verses we avoid because they simply do not fit into the theme of grace and salvation through Yeshua, as we understand them.

We should be careful about this, since it was written, *"Forever O Lord, thy word is settled in [the] heavens"* (Psalm 119:89).

A key word to aid understanding of the "get wealth" passage is the Hebrew root term

"ahsah"

A concordance shows that it means do, make, or work. It was used of the Lord's creative work in the Genesis account; along with the word

"create"

It is found in Genesis 1:26, when God said;

> *Let us make man in our image.*
> *That verse shows a plural form for*
> *'let us.'*

It must surely refer to the image of God, as noted in the reproductive process, inherent in the man, the woman, and God.

Genesis 5:3 indicates that Adam begat a son in his own likeness; after his image.

In Genesis 2:18, it was written about the woman's creation:

> *I will make him an help meet for him.*

In both cases the word make is used. Yet, in the example about the woman, the terms I will make in the Hebrew and the English are both singular.

The only way to reconcile the verses is to know that this chronological order is not event specific, and that in the case of the creative act regarding man and woman, it is the same God. Unless of course, we are willing to admit that a singular God created the woman, and a multiple god person created the man. Huh? Wouldn't that information really help the women libbers? Ha! Ha!

Joking aside, we admit that the term "make" in regard to God's ability, can also mean create. The examples given are evidence enough.

*We must also recognize that the Lord God
can enable His children to "make wealth,"
in order to establish His covenant
as He promised, for the forefathers
of the children of Israel.*

ישוע

Spoke about Blasphemy

Chapter 16

Jesus Spoke About Blasphemy

We would rather not have to discuss such a delicate subject as blasphemy, but Jesus had to deal with so much resistance at times, he must have surely been angered or agitated, especially after having ministered miracles or healings on behalf of the multitudes and then entering into a teaching session. The next thing you know some religious person was challenging his every word or action.

In Matthew 12:24-39, *Jesus' detractors were present, and had became so verbally abusive and vociferous they had accused him of practicing demonic matters, due to his huge success in expelling demons and bringing deliverance into people's lives.*

Were they just jealous of his fame and authority in those things? Or, were they feeling guilty because of their lack in such matters? Was an itinerant rabbi grabbing the religious spotlight, and showing what ought to be happening in the ministry? Were those leaders becoming fearful for their "place" in the sight of the populace? I can only say that Jesus was bringing the "movement" of God into people's lives and doing a great work. He was bringing God nearer than the fingers on ones hand.

But, his critics were not so impressed. They accused and dishonored him greatly. Jesus considered them blasphemers, since they did not credit the finger of God with healing and deliverance in his ministry. Rather, some Pharisees accused him of demonic activity. Maybe that's why Jesus reacted so strongly against what he considered a generation of hypocritical Pharisee's. He felt that denial of God's work among His people, and attribution of such to Satan, was indeed blasphemy.

Whenever religious people attribute healing, deliverance, and miracles, among the people of God, to the work of demons, it is a very serious charge, and is not to be taken lightly. Jesus labelled such hateful and vocal hypocrisy as blasphemy of the Holy Spirit (Matthew 12:32).

Just what is blasphemy anyway?

The Greek Bible term is usually (blas-fay-me'-ah, 3988), and generally refers to vilification against God. The Greek root form can mean speaking evil against man or God. In the Old Testament or

(Hebrew Bible), the terms blaspheme, blasphemed, blasphemeth, and blaspemies/blasphemy all appear in the English text.

There are several Hebrew words used in the texts, but the basic meaning of all of them is akin to scorn, puncture, perforate, hack with words, revile. The most probable word to describe Jesus antagonists and their speech against him, would be the Hebrew

$$גָּדַף$$

That word is also used in a Hebrew translation version of Matthew 12:32, It is likewise found in 2Kings 19:6, Ezekiel 20:27, and Psalm 44:16.

In our first example the servants of the king of Assyria blasphemed the Lord. In our second example, the fathers of the elders of Israel had blasphemed the Lord, committing a trespass against Him. The last example in Psalm 44:16, relates how the enemies of Israel reproached and blasphemed the children of God.

These verses indicate with certainty that the term blaspheme can be to speak against or scorn God or His children. ...A serious matter indeed. At this point, it seems to me, a person is treading on dangerous ground, or a slippery slope. It has been said that, only fools rush in where angels fear to tread.

Just how serious is the matter of blasphemy?

Jesus didn't pull any punches when dealing with the issue. His words were like a heavyweight boxer who was hitting back at his opponent with knock out power. Listen to his words.

> *But he that shall blaspheme against the Holy Ghost hath never forgiveness, but is in danger of eternal damnation. Because they said, He hath an unclean spirit* (Mark 3:29-30).

We see from his words, that to accuse someone who is full of the Spirit of God doing mighty works, and say they are operating under demon forces, is what those leaders were guilty of doing. They had crossed the line of decency and logic, and become blind in their zeal against Jesus. He warned them of danger.

The possibility of never being forgiven existed since they were demeaning the mighty work of God and His servant. They were in danger of eternal damnation. *If that was the case when the Son of*

Man, God's last day spokesman was here, what shall we say about now when he is in heaven, seated at the Father's right hand, and we are in the dispensation of the Holy Ghost? Is it the justice or decision of God that such persons have went beyond the laws of faith and grace of God?

Considering the redemptive work of God regarding forgiveness has been completed by the actions of Jesus on the tree, and that he stated it is finished, how then shall we escape justice if we speak evil against the works of God, performed because of His Spirit in this world? Didn't the resurrection of Jesus substantiate any claims on his behalf, whether his words or deeds were true? Hasn't God borne witness of the one whom He sent into this world? Are we not believers who accept him as our substitute?

It would be different if Jesus were a fake or charlatan as some pretenders have been. But, God verified among many witnesses about the authority of Jesus. *"He went about doing good and healing all that were oppressed of the devil, for God was with him."*

For that reason and many others, people should be very careful to not be offensive to God with cruel words and heartless vocal comments. It's all right to be a "fruit inspector," of a person's life or character, but it's wrong to be a constant critic or judge over the mighty work of God.

How sad it must be to the Lord, when He hears folk blaspheme and deny His work, or attribute it to demons, a devil, or an unclean spirit. The law of eternal damnation isn't just for unbelievers; it holds a future for religionists who are guilty of the sin of blasphemy.

I recall some powerful words that Jesus once said, as reported by Matthew 10:28,

> *"...rather fear Him which is able to destroy both soul and body in hell."*

Jesus warned with a very serious tone about blasphemy.

He mentioned of an ultimate destruction in hell for those guilty of such vile and negative speech. He knew that words could defile, condemn, or justify in the sight of God.

Such warnings from Jesus, if doing nothing else, should cause us all to walk more humbly and reverently in the presence of God.

Glossary of Terms

When reading through this book, one may encounter some terms that are unfamiliar to the reader. I have listed some of them below and they will appear in the same order as chapters develop, rather than alphabetical order.

Sabbath-Shabbat; The normal day of rest in Judaism, the 7th day with a corrected Hebrew to English rendering

Observant; A Jew who practices and tries to keep the Laws of God

Synagogue; A New Testament Greek term referring to the place where Jewish worshippers assembled

Ecclessia; A Greek Testament word which represents the "assembly of called out ones"

Mikdash; A very old Hebrew Bible term which represents the "Holy Temple" [Exodus 25:8,

2Chronicles 36:17]

Bar Mitzvah; A symbol and celebration of the Jewish male's willingness to accept the yoke of the kingdom upon themselves, or the full responsibility of an adult Jew

Bat Mitzvah; Same as above except it relates to the feminine nature

Edersheim; A Jew who became a Christian, scholar and author. Well known for his writings about Jesus

Didaskalos; A Greek New Testament word for "teacher"

Pesach; A Hebrew Bible word for "Passover"

Berit Milah; A covenant cut in Judaism; circumcision

Avot-Pirkei Avot; Saying of the Fathers, ethical and moral teachings of some 60 Jewish sages

Tekton; A Greek New Testament word for "carpenter, craftsman"

Talmud; Generally speaking, this term refers

rather to the Babylonian Talmud, rather than the smaller Jerusalem Talmud. The Babylonian Talmud is a collection of the extensive discussions and interpretations by scholars of the Mishnah, which means repetition or teaching

Judah ha Nassi; Jewish teacher, par excellence. 135–217 C.E., known among Jews as "our holy rabbi"

Yosef; The Hebrew name for the English "Joseph"

Miriam; The Hebrew name for the English "Mary"

Shema; A Jewish declaration of faith in the One God, with verses found in Deuteronomy 6:4-9

Elohim; A Hebrew bible word, which has various meanings, including gods, idols, false gods, judges, and the One True God

Gentile; A non Jew

Septuagint; The oldest Greek version of the bible, which in Latin relates to 70 [translators ?]. Maybe used by Jews in Alexandria, Egypt, and made around 285 B.C. to 247–288 B.C.

Glossary

Peyot; A Hebrew word that refers to what is known as sideburns on the head and near the ears, and which God commanded Jewish males not to cut

Rabbi; A word meaning "my master," or "my teacher"

Semikhah; Jewish ordination, before one can decide practical questions of Jewish law, and involving the "laying on of hands"

Great Assembly; A group of 120 sages who led the Jewish people at the beginning of the Second Temple era. This included the last three prophets of Judaism, which were Haggai, Zechariah, and Malachi

Bat kol; Daughter of a voice, a Divine decree issued from heaven to decide a matter

Evasive synonym; Using a word that means the same in order to avoid overmuch use of the primary word. Example: The word "God" is replaced by the word "heaven" or the Kingdom of Heaven instead of the Kingdom of God. This avoids profaning the Divine name and keeps Exodus 20:7 from being violated, according to some Jewish thinking

Aramaic; A Shemitic language, but not

Hebrew. It was the official language of the Persian Empire, and became the tongue of exiled Jews of Babylon after the destruction of Jerusalem

Tzion; The corrected Hebrew to English transliteration of the word "Zion". A hill on the Temple Mount in Jerusalem

Olam ha zeh; A Hebrew term meaning "this world"

Olam ha bah; A Hebrew term meaning "the world to come"

Segulah; A biblical word translated as "peculiar" [people] in the KJV, but meaning "treasured" people

Pharisee; One of three major sects in Israel before the destruction of the Temple in 70AD. It teachings formed the basis of rabbinic Judaism. The root word of Pharisees means "separate/separatist

Semite/Semitic; A scholarly misnomer based on the Greek form of the name of "Shem," one of three sons of Noah/Noach, by whom the world was repopulated after the flood. His true name was Shem, and implies the Shemitic line from whence the Hebrews came

Glossary

Josephus; A Jewish historian of the first century, and soldier of Jewish forces. He surrendered to the Romans and aided them. For that reason he was considered by many as a "traitor"

Antiquities; Works and writings attributed to Josephus to explain history and antiquites of the Jewish people and the war with Rome

Scribe; An ancient profession requiring one to read and write, and a person specially trained to write a Torah scroll in a very pious manner

Tzizit; The singular form of a Hebrew word for tassel or fringe [KJV], the plural is tzitziot [Numbers 15:38-42]

Nedarim; The word means "vows." It's also the name of a tractate in the Mishnah.

Kraspeda; The Greek New Testament word for Tzizit and translated "border" [of his garment]

Dunamis; A Greek word meaning "power." It is similar in meaning to dynamic, dynamo, dynamite, etc.

Teras; A Greek New Testament word meaning "wonder" or "omen"

Glossary

Seimion; A Greek New Testament word meaning "sign"

Therapyouo; A Greek New Testament word sometimes rendered "healing"

Rapha; This Hebrew word means "heal"

Avraham; The Hebrew name of Abraham

Yitzhak; The Hebrew name of Isaac

Yaakov; The Hebrew name of Jacob

Yehovah Yireh; The bible translation is "The Lord will see"

Golgotha; The word means "skull." It is a Chaldean word incorporated into Hebrew. A knoll near Jerusalem

Parable; A Greek New Testament word used in the gospels as a teaching tool by Jesus

Mashal; The Hebrew term for the Greek word parable. Rendered Proverb by English translators

Asaph; A writer of some Psalms, rewritten by David, according to Jewish tradition

Glossary

Rabbi Hirsch; 1808–1888, German theologian and Rabbi, as well as author of biblical commentaries

Maimonides; Moses ben Maimon, 1135-1204, foremost intellectual figure of medevial Judaism. Author of numerous writings

JPS; Three initials for Jewish Publication Society

Bar Kochba; A Jewish leader in Palestine who led the revolt against the Romans in AD

Ben Sira; In the second century before the common era [BCE], Ben Sira of Jerusalem wrote an apocrypha in Hebrew which his grandson translated into Greek. it was a collection of wisdom, and ethics

Luther; 1483–1546, German religious reformer and the founder of Protestantism

Rabbi Akiva; 40–135 AD, Jewish sage and martyr in Palestine. Founded the great rabbinical school at Jaffa. He was flayed alive in martyrdom

Malkenu; A Hebrew term meaning "our King." It is used in many Jewish prayers and liturgy

Avinu; A Hebrew word meaning "our

Father," and used in numerous prayers and Jewish liturgy

Yom Kippur; The Day of Atonement in Judaism

Kidush ha Shem; sanctification of the name

Vilna Gaon; Rabbi Eliyahu of Vilna. The most influential Jewish leader in modern history [1720-1797]. His fame, knowledge, and righteousness caused him to become known as the Vilna Gaon. The word Gaon means "genius."

Tanach/Tanakh/TNK- The first letter of each Hebrew section of the Jewish Bible; Torah, Naviim, and Ktuvim, form the consonants TNK. This is known by Jews throughout the world, and sometime called Nahk

Panim el Panim; Hebrew for face to face, and reveals how God talked with Moses.

Peh el Peh; Mouth to mouth, another biblical phrase for God speaking to Moses without dream or vision

Mammon; An ancient Chaldean loan word incorporated into the Hebrew language, with a figurative meaning of "wealth" or "money"

Resources

Look for our books and resources on Kindle and Amazon. If you have enjoyed or learned from Ronald's book "The Real Jesus" leave a comment or review on Amazon and rate it. Find us on Facebook too!

Other titles by Ronald L Drown include: "Jesus and Our Jewish Roots," "Hebrew Prayers," and the Book of Discovery ... "Nuggets."

For instructional material, books, publications and other media resources contact:

Ancient Truth Publishing
PO Box 366894
Bonita Springs, FL 34136 or
Visit: www.AncientTruthPublishing.com

To order copies of this book, or to learn more about books and resources from Pastor Ronald L Drown, visit the website at: www.Jesus-About.com.

About the Author

Rev. Ronald Drown teaches modern (Sephardic) Hebrew to leaders, and in small group church and seminar settings. The late Robert L Lindsay, Scholar, Author, Founder of "The Jerusalem Perspective," and Pastor in Jerusalem for 47 years, highly commended Rev. Ronald Drown for his translation of "The Gospel of Mark," from Hebrew to English. His knowledge of the Hebrew Biblical text has both practicality and depth.

His familiarity with Jewish traditions which relate well to the Christian faith, allow him to provide rich learning experiences to the Christian community, enhancing the understanding of their religious roots and enriching Biblical studies. His working knowledge of the Greek New Testament is also a valuable help to students of the Bible.

Pastor Ron Drown has founded "Yad-El" ...a nonprofit ministry in Florida, with a vision for teaching in the Hebrew and Jewish traditions to the church, and a mission to help hurting people, needy children, the elderly, and the underprivileged. His focus is particular to the Jewish people, as he has a heart for Israel, and provides for ministries such as the Wings of Eagles, who regularly feeds and transports Jewish families back to their homeland from the former Soviet Union.

Rev. Drown's Vision Includes ... Evangelism and Ministry, through the use of seminars, media, internet, publishing, radio and television... to instruct and train, while promoting Gods love, and the Gospel of Jesus Christ.

Rev. Drown Is Available ... To assist local leaders and pastors as he shares the word of God, drawing from his many years of experience, helping churches and encouraging them through teaching and preaching.

If you would like him to visit your assembly, event, or fellowship, he is available for preaching, teaching, speaking, or seminar events. Please feel free to contact him through his offices in Southwest Florida

YAD-EL Ministries P.O. Box 366936, Bonita Springs, FL 34136, or visit: www.Jesus-About.com. Email: YadelMinistries@Yahoo.com